Peopled Leadership

Peopled Leadership

Growing People and Transforming Organizations

R. Stewart Mayers
Jennifer M. Anderson
Todd Williams

ROWMAN & LITTLEFIELD
Lanham • Boulder • New York • London

Published by Rowman & Littlefield
An imprint of The Rowman & Littlefield Publishing Group, Inc.
4501 Forbes Boulevard, Suite 200, Lanham, Maryland 20706
www.rowman.com

86-90 Paul Street, London EC2A 4NE, United Kingdom

British Library Cataloguing in Publication Information Available

Library of Congress Cataloging-in-Publication Data Available

Names: Mayers, R. Stewart, 1959- author. | Anderson, Jennifer M., 1971- author. | Williams, Todd, 1963- author.
Title: Peopled leadership : growing people and transforming organizations / R. Stewart Mayers, Jennifer M. Anderson, Todd Williams.
Description: Lanham, Maryland : Rowman & Littlefield Publishing, [2023] | Includes bibliographical references and index. | Summary: "Peopled Leadership empowers others to lead, be innovative, engage in collaboration, solve complex problems, and further outcomes"—Provided by publisher.
Identifiers: LCCN 2022047453 (print) | LCCN 2022047454 (ebook) | ISBN 9781475868418 (cloth) | ISBN 9781475868425 (paperback) | ISBN 9781475868432 (epub)
Subjects: LCSH: Leadership. | Organizational effectiveness.
Classification: LCC HD57.7 .M3944 2023 (print) | LCC HD57.7 (ebook) | DDC 658.4/092—dc23/eng/20230111
LC record available at https://lccn.loc.gov/2022047453
LC ebook record available at https://lccn.loc.gov/2022047454

This book is dedicated to my wife, Mary Ellen, for her constant support of my work and to my colleagues in the Department of Educational Instruction and Leadership and the Office of Teacher Education Services at Southeastern Oklahoma State University who helped me learn how to be a leader.
—RSM

I do this work on behalf of my two children, John and Jordan, as well as those who believed in me and continue to do so. For every child who was told you would not make it, you can, and this is also for you!
—JMA

This book is dedicated to my family.
—CTW

Contents

Acknowledgments

An endeavor such as this book is truly a team effort. We are indebted to Sally Jackson, secretary/program assistant for the Department of Educational Instruction and Leadership; Jennifer Arnold, coordinator of Teacher Education Services; and Kelli Norman, data collection specialist for Teacher Education Services (all at Southeastern Oklahoma State University) for assuming extra duties to allow us the time to research, write, and edit this book. We also wish to express our deep appreciation to the following accomplished leaders who provided endorsements for *Peopled Leadership*: Dr. Sally J. Zepeda, professor of Educational Administration and Policy, University of Georgia; Mr. Duane Merideth, superintendent, Durant Independent School District, Durant, Oklahoma; Rev. Chris Dowd, senior minister, Christ United Methodist Church, Plano, Texas; and Sean Covey, President, FranklinCovey Education.

An academic department's success is attributable to many factors beginning with the faculty and staff who comprise it. We are deeply appreciative of the support of our departmental colleagues during the journey of writing this book. We are also indebted to Dr. Thomas Newsom, president of Southeastern Oklahoma State University, and Dr. Teresa Golden, vice president of academic affairs at Southeastern, for their constant support of our work. We are indebted to Professor Jack Ousey of the Department of Art, Communication, and Theatre who brought to life the *Peopled Leadership Model* through his creativity and considerable artistic talents.

We also wish to acknowledge the support of our families for their patience and understanding during the long hours required for a project of this magnitude.

Introduction

As a leader, nothing is more gratifying than knowing that your organization is headed in a good direction. As a "peopled" leader, nothing is more gratifying than knowing you have played a role in helping team members accomplish their goals, thereby providing the conditions under which the organization succeeds. Trust, humility, and empathy are essential ingredients for leaders to be able to create the climate necessary for those they lead to experience autonomy, to make decisions about their professional goals and practices, and to take the risks necessary for individual and organizational growth to occur. When this type of distributed leadership model emerges, people feel empowered to think and act on a higher level and see things they may not have seen before.

The 21st century has presented and continues to present challenges for leaders that are unprecedented. Evolving technology presents new and more efficient solutions to existing tasks but simultaneously, has created a host of new challenges to address. New interpretations of existing laws, such as Title VII and Title IX, are rewriting the legal landscape in which leaders work. The ongoing effects of the COVID-19 pandemic continue to stretch scarce resources, adding to the pressures of being an effective leader.

Zepeda and Lanoue (2021) asserted that 21st-century leaders provide the most effective leadership by "connecting with and through shared values; prioritizing what matters most: people making time to recalibrate, modeling strength, vulnerability, and honesty; and focusing on the future." In "Leadership Models: The Theory and the Practice," Caredda (2020) examined 120 different models of leadership. These models are divided into six categories: theoretical, competency based, values based, effectiveness based, purpose based, and applicative. To address the 21st-century problems facing schools, we propose a new kind of leadership model, one that is people based. We call it *Peopled Leadership*.

Peopled leaders remain true to their goals of serving others even during times of consternation brought on by situational factors that can complicate matters and make the desired outcome something that is beneficial for all involved. When leaders are thrust into 21st-century situations that require thoughtful reflection and careful consideration of numerous issues that are applying enormous pressure, the idea of focusing on someone else can serve as a huge distraction, especially considering the compressed timeframe in which many of today's leadership decisions are made. Effective leadership requires the building of trust, which allows organization members to think more about the needs of others as well as about themselves.

Peopled Leadership is a new model of leadership we are proposing for 21st-century organizations facing today's tumultuous environment of rushed deadlines and ever-evolving challenges. *Peopled Leadership* comprises three phases: People Oriented, People Empowered, and People Transformed. Phase one provides tools for the leader to use to build trust and transparency in the organization, two conditions necessary to forge the bonds for a team-focused climate that allows the creativity necessary for the organization to realize its vision and mission. Phase two, People Empowered, describes how leaders can break down barriers to the professional growth of team members on whom they depend for their success. The third phase, people-transformed leadership, provides discussion about the hard work of maintaining the momentum created by a workplace of transformed people.

Chapter 1 introduces the *Peopled Leadership* model and why we believe it is the answer to the challenges of 21st-century leadership. Chapter 2 discusses the initial phase of *Peopled Leadership*, People Oriented. The reader is introduced to the research literature about the need for shared values as a prerequisite for building trust. Research is presented to inform how peopled leaders build trust as a first step to creating the foundation necessary for gaining transparency and the ability to be vulnerable with organization members and for setting the conditions to take the necessary risks for personal and organizational growth. Chapter 3 presents the second phase of *Peopled Leadership*, People Empowered. Research on humility, empowerment, and autonomy provides the underpinnings for strategies that peopled leaders use to promote the work and skills of those they lead. As a result of these strategies, peopled leaders create additional leaders.

Chapter 4 provides the reader detailed information about the third and final phase of the *Peopled Leadership* model, People Transformed. This chapter provides a detailed description of emotional intelligence and servant leadership as the theoretical bases of People Transformed. This chapter also presents the ways in which a transformed organization is ideally equipped to manage change, create an environment of listening, and solve problems. Chapters 2 through 4 conclude with a case study and set of discussion questions to further the reader's understanding of *Peopled Leadership*.

Chapter 5 introduces the reader to the heart of *Peopled Leadership*, the active practice of gratitude. Through the practice of gratitude, the peopled leader is uniquely able to build cohesiveness and synergy in an organization. Through the practice of gratitude, peopled leaders are able to facilitate and nurture a sense of belonging in their professional organizations. Chapter 6 discusses the application of *Peopled Leadership* to the thorny issues of accountability leaders invariably must address. The final chapter ends with a "Coda for Peopled Leaders," which provides practical guidance for being a peopled leader in the 21st-century environment by taking care of oneself.

Why, with at least 120 models of leadership already "out there," do we need another? The challenges facing 21st-century leadership continue to evolve at a frightening pace. The key to successfully leading in this environment is people. That's why we need *Peopled Leadership*.

REFERENCES

Caredda, S. (2020, August 21). *Leadership models: The theory and the practice.* https://sergiocaredda.eu/organisation/leadership-models-the-theory-and-the-practice

Zepeda, S. J., & Lanoue, P. D. (2021). *A leadership guide to navigating the unknown: New narratives amid COVID-19.* Routledge.

Chapter 1

Peopled Leadership

Why This Model Is Essential for 21st-Century Leaders

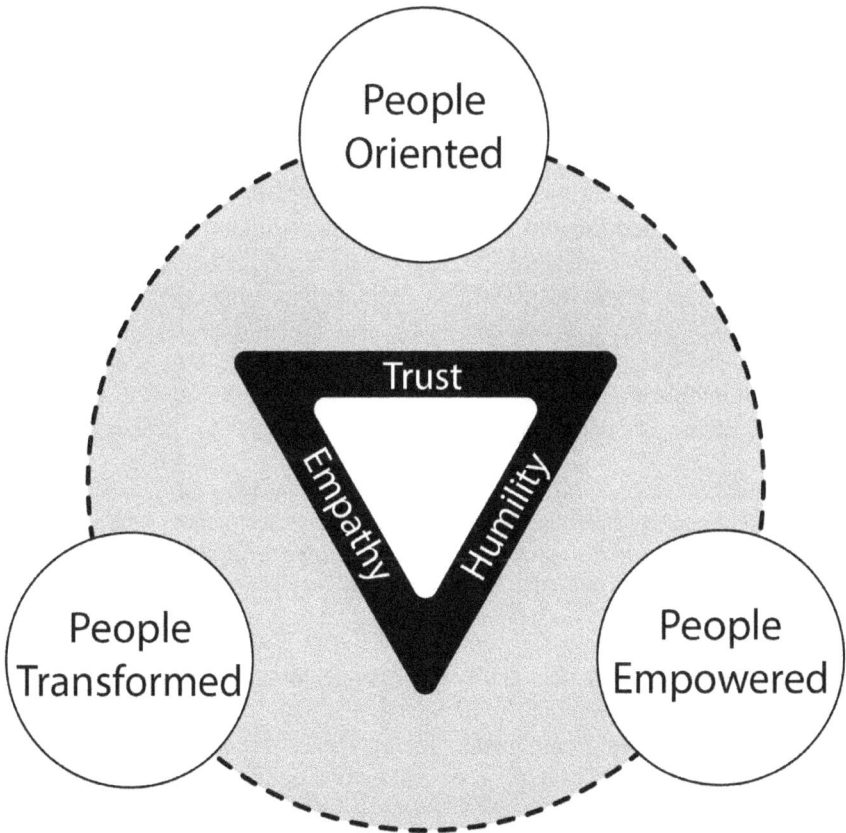

People Oriented

Trust

Empathy

Humility

People Transformed

People Empowered

Fig. 1.1. *Peopled Leadership:* Base Model. *Jack Ousey.*

Leaders operate in complex environments, have immense responsibilities, and face tremendous demands. Systems, organizations, and institutions are not static. Zepeda and Lanoue (2021) reported that "examining and amplifying change and the complexities of decision making" supports leaders "in the introspection and rethinking that support short- and long-term planning for whatever the 'new normal' brings to bear" (p. xii). We call this quality "organizational agility."

The forces that affect organizations evolve based on numerous and ever-changing factors and with ever-growing speed. According to *The Flux Report* (Right Management, 2014), 98% of organizations have experienced major organizational change in the last five years. Further, in their study, 91% of human resources decision-makers believe potential employees will be recruited/selected based on their ability to manage change.

Maxwell (2019) states, "Good leaders adapt. They shift. They don't remain static. This has always been true, but it's never been more obvious than today" (p. 5). The ability to shift an organization's focus, climate, and operations has never been greater than in today's challenging environment. Developing this ability begins with becoming a people-oriented leader. Thus, we offer a new model of leadership that puts people first and at the heart of all an organization does, be it a school, a business, or a religious organization: *Peopled Leadership.*

The need for adaptability is true as well. Addressing the educational environment, Kaplan and Owings (2015) assert that "Without a doubt, the principalship is an important, intensive, and complex job. Schools need capable leaders who can rally faculty, staff, students, parents, and community members to invest their time and effort in educating all children" (p. 2).

Leaders have tremendous responsibility, and policies that seek to hold them accountable are not enough. Rather than policies, Tooley (2021) argues that the culture of leadership must change:

> Policy shifts won't be sufficient on their own—they must be accompanied by shifts in culture and communication around what it means to be a school leader. Without a new approach to . . . leadership, we'll continue to struggle to attract and retain the talent necessary to secure the best possible outcomes . . . (para. 5)

Fullan (2008) contends that "Powerful change forces have certainly bombarded . . . [leaders], making life more onerous but also containing glimpses of new interdependent components" (p. 1). He asserts that these new interdependent components require new leadership models and new leadership frameworks.

Managing change in a 21st-century environment requires a new, dynamic leadership model that addresses the open system's complexities leaders face. Heifetz and Linsky (2004) assert that such challenges and complexities require leaders "to learn and adapt new ways of engaging in shared leadership opportunities" (p. 33).

Addressing the education environment, Levin and Fullan (2008) contend that "Schools are expected to be all things to all people" (p. 293). This expectation is part of the complexity of educational leadership. Other complexities current education leaders face include funding shortages and complex financial conditions, shifts in student demographics and populations, political context of education and education reform, increased socioeconomic impacts, staff and educator retention and shortages, technological innovations and learning modalities, student and employee mental and emotional health needs, school safety, open borders and world connectivity, and even globalized health issues.

In addition to these changes and shifts, education accountability policies, the need for school reform, and the focus on educational improvement also require a new leadership model. Safer et al. (2010) contend that "The demands for improvement and reform require attention to innovative leadership models" (para. 1).

Because leadership has changed, so have the required skills of leaders. Leaders can no longer follow antiquated practices and leadership models and expect new, transformed results. New frameworks, strategies, and approaches are needed to navigate new waters and the dynamics of an ever-changing environment. Institutions and systems are representative of real life, and real life is centered on change.

According to Hersey (1984), "Real life situations are never static. They're in a constant state of change" (p. 15). Change and the ability to navigate, adapt, and leverage it require a commitment to the very people who implement the change and those affected by it. Wong and Davey (2007) assert that "New types of leaders are needed to create new futures" (p. 1). Fullan (2008) argues:

> There is no question that the role of school leader has become more complex and in many ways "undoable" under current conditions. My solution . . . is not to strive for stability, but to reposition the role of the principal so that school leaders can be a force for school and system transformation. (p. 3)

Peopled Leadership is that new dynamic model aimed at creating new leaders and new futures. It is people centric and people oriented with a focus on developing and empowering others.

Peopled Leadership provides the much-needed shift from accountability and outcome-focused–driven leadership behaviors to behaviors that focus on people, while assuring accountability and improvement. According to Heifetz and Linsky (2004):

> Policymakers are demanding performance accountability measures for students and educators that bring into question deeply held notions of good teaching, good learning, and success in the classroom; these accountability measures also force us to face our long-standing acceptance of the wide gaps in achievement between rich and poor students and between white and minority students. The kind of leadership that can fashion new and better responses to those local realities needs to come from many places within classrooms, districts, and communities. (p. 37)

While accountability measures are not new, many of the policies and inputs into our systems are.

Peopled Leadership is a model that orients a leader's focus on people and their commitment to the people, schools, organizations, communities, and institutions they serve. This new model empowers others to lead, be innovative, engage in collaboration, solve complex problems, and further outcomes. The result of *Peopled Leadership* is the transformation of people and the transformation of practices that mitigate the complexities intrinsic to the improvement of the organization and the achievement of desired and needed outcomes.

PHASES OF THE MODEL

The term *leadership* is generally used in two ways. In its most common use, leadership is simply being the leader or head of an organization and describes all the various activities of a leader's daily assumed responsibilities. According to Jackson (2021), "Leadership was created by the institution, it's designed to maintain the institution, not transform it" (p. 1). While both proactive, vision-directed leadership and reactive management are required of leaders, true leadership focuses on people. Transformation begins when leaders place people at the heart of their practices.

Current leadership studies have come to focus on the proactive dimensions of leadership. Leaders are key facilitators in developing a vision for the direction of the organization; in developing effective, collaborative relationships with various stakeholders; and in coordinating the efforts and growth of others in distributed leadership. Mintzberg (2004) argues that "Leadership is not about making clever decisions and doing bigger deals, least of all for personal gain. It is about energizing other people to make good decisions and do better things" (p. 16).

The first phase of *Peopled Leadership* is People Oriented. As we define the people-oriented phase, people are the heart of the organization. All accomplishments of the organization depend on the people. They are treated with respect and dignity, properly equipped, and supported to enable the organization to establish and meet goals and to realize a vision. The focus of People Oriented is on the development of people in the organization. Glickman et al. (2018) asserts the best way to improve teachers is to equip them to make better decisions. That is true for all people in any organization. A function of leadership in the people-oriented facet is to improve the organization by guiding the people of the organization into growth and self-actualization through productive, professional, collaborative relationships with others. That improvement begins with establishing trust.

The second phase of *Peopled Leadership* is People Empowered. People Empowered are trusted, resourced, respected, and vision driven. They have been provided with the autonomy to make decisions about their own professional development and to become active participants in the decision-making for the organization. People Empowered can be described as working in collaborative ways to foster distributed leadership within an organization. This facet begins when the leader moves aside to allow the people of the organization to perform in self-directed work, in reflective decision-making, and in various levels of distributed leadership. People Empowered takes a great amount of work, collaboration, capacity building, and trust. This is the facet of *Peopled Leadership* where dynamic collaboration and growth in the organization are exhibited.

The final phase of *Peopled Leadership* is People Transformed. People Transformed are people whose self-image and perception of and commitment to the organization have been positively changed through joint efforts of the organization's members. Transformed people have relationships that allow them to take calculated risks with internal and external stakeholders to achieve agreed-upon outcomes for the organization. In the people-transformed phase, the community outside the organization is included in positive, collaborative relationships that are instrumental in achieving the mission and goals of the organization. With transformed people, the vision not only drives organizational achievement but also leads and drives community improvement.

ESSENTIAL THREE ELEMENTS

Trust Is the Foundation of Leadership

Trust is a feature found in some leadership models (Bartell & Bartell, 2016; Dräger, n.d.; Zenger & Folkman, 2009). The Dräger (n.d.) model, WeLEAD, is one of the few in which trust is a central feature. A unique feature of *Peopled Leadership* is that trust forms the very foundation of the model. Without trust, leadership that puts people first cannot occur.

Bencsik et al. (2020) describe trust as "a very complex construct" that has been "defined in many different ways" (p. 30). Paliszkiewicz (2010, as cited in Paliszkiewicz et al., 2015), defined trust as

> The belief that another party a) will not act in a way that is harmful to the trusting firm, b) will act in such a way that it is beneficial to the trusting firm, c) will act reliably, and d) will behave or respond in a predictable and mutually acceptable manner. (p. 20)

Using this definition, an effective leader is one who works for the benefit of the organization, is reliable, and is consistent in behaviors, both actions and words. However, the benefits of trust in an organization are more profound. Geier (2016) found that when leaders are trusted, members of the organization believe group performance is improved. Huntsman and Greer (2019) concluded that a lack of trust in leadership tends to be detrimental to both internal and external stakeholders of the organization. Deep levels of trust create the conditions that allow team members to be transparent with one another, permit risk taking, and promote collaboration.

Transparency and Leadership

A first and necessary step to establishing trust in an organization is creating a climate of transparency. Whitehall et al. (2021) define transparency as "presenting one's authentic self to others, which promotes trust among followers" (p. 116). Farrell (2016) quotes the *Business Dictionary*, which defines transparency as the "lack of hidden agendas, accompanied by the availability of full information required for collaboration, cooperation, and collective decision making" (p. 445). We believe transparency is also the practice of acting and communicating in such a way that members of the organization consider themselves valued, respected, and included. Employees particularly desire for transparency in decision-making (Farrell, 2016).

Transparency requires leaders to be consistent and open. Decisions should be made based on stable data and appropriate input from stakeholders and then explained with as much detail as is permissible. Leaders who are transparent demonstrate their interest in others' point of view. Interest begins with listening to those for whom the leader is responsible. According to Greenleaf (2002), "Listening is an attitude, an attitude toward people and what they are trying to express" (p. 313).

Transparency provides team members with needed knowledge about resources that are available for the work of the organization as well as their individual projects. Team members are better able to plan their work and focus their efforts. Members also have reason to believe those resources are being used to their best advantage to help the organization reach its goals.

Risk-Taking

One of the by-products of trust in an organization is the willingness, even the eagerness, to take risks. With deep levels of trust, members of the organization think outside the box, making individuals and the group more effective problem solvers.

In the era of COVID, widespread unrest, and deep division in society, it is more important than ever for organizations to be able to solve problems quickly. Nienaber et al. (2015) concluded that a necessary component to trust is the ability to risk being vulnerable. Lindell et al. (2016) found that under conditions favorable to innovation (including trust), leaders not only tended to take risks with creative thinking; they also did so across disciplines as well as within their own discipline. In their landmark study of teachers and supervisors, Zepeda and Ponticell (1998) identified risk-taking as a key to individual professional growth and by extension, the growth of the organization:

> Freedom to fail was an important condition needed to move teachers from willingness to change to action. Change requires risk, a "venture to uncertainty." Risking taking, however, does not come easily, as it makes the risk taker vulnerable. To experiment with new ideas, teachers . . . expressed a need to feel free from fear of rebuke, rejection, or retaliation if the experiment failed. (p. 82)

The experience of the Department of Educational Instruction and Leadership has reflected the lessons learned in the research concerning risk-taking. When members of the organization trust each other enough to take risks, a synergy is built that combines the skills, knowledge, and experience of the group members, creating a robust creative and robust problem-solving apparatus. In a word, collaboration becomes second nature.

Collaboration

The third feature of organizations in which a deep level of trust has been created is the natural dependency on collaboration. Trust is essential for team building. Zenger and Folkman (2002) assert that "Teams without trust suffer from conflicts and competition between team members. It is easy to talk about trust, but it tends to be an elusive quality of many leaders" (p. 198). What are the characteristics of leaders who have built a high level of trust with their people? Leaders who build trust in their organizations are themselves transparent, consistent, and selfless.

When a leader is transparent, members of the organization know what to expect. Decision-making has a natural flow in which members of the organization are involved, engaged, and invested. Further, members of the organization have the freedom to become more transparent themselves, building trust in one another. This leads to increased capacity for problem solving and conflict resolution.

Consistency is also a necessary component to *Peopled Leadership*. Consistency helps remove the possibility of "gotcha" moments because members of the organization know what to expect. They know how others are likely to react to a given stimulus. Consistency also provides a "safe space" for members to take risks and to provide the support necessary for resilience in difficult times. Finally, leadership for collaboration is selfless. This means leaders building collaborative teams redistribute power. Hoy and Miskel (2013) put it this way: "When work is complex, experts or professionals are required, and with them come demands for autonomy to make decisions based on the basis of authority or ideology. To be most successful, [leaders] . . . need to share power with professionals" (p. 242).

Resources

All organizations need resources. However, resources are scarce, and strong, peopled leaders are good stewards of the organization's resources. Perhaps the most important resources in any organization are the people themselves. In their study of leadership, Zenger and Folkman (2002) identify 16 behaviors their participants identified with effective leaders. Some of these are problem solving, innovating, promoting a spirit of continuous improvement, inspiring and developing others to achieve high performance, creating a climate of collaboration, and facilitating needed change. These traits require the effective leader to also be a quality developer and manager of needed resources.

Some needed resources are obvious. Others are more subtle. Some of the more obvious include technology, facilities, and time. Effective organizations depend on technology for communication, productivity, resource management, marketing, and much more. Without technology, workplaces come to a standstill. Although meeting platforms have lessened the need, many organizations still require physical facilities to provide safe environments for the organization's operations. Perhaps the most precious resource is time. Since everyone has the same amount available, the effective leader works to protect the organization members' time to ensure every minute is spent wisely. Meetings need to be crisp and productive, taking only the time needed. Unnecessary meetings should be avoided or replaced with emails. Effective leaders have the trust of their people; their people know their time will be protected, not wasted.

Other more subtle resources necessary for success include trust, humility, empathy, and emotional intelligence that permeates the organization. These resources are essential for building the positive, supportive, and energizing climate required for success individually and as an organization. Like their more obvious counterparts, these more subtle resources must be spent wisely and genuinely.

Knowledge

Trust and sufficient resources provide the tools to create the synergy required for the organization to create and extend the knowledge to meet its goals and fulfill its mission. Knowledge is generated through learning. Kelly (2018) believes that "professional and personal growth comes only from learning . . . [which comes] in many forms—from feedback, colleagues, personal relationships, successes and failures, research and study, and everything in between" (p. 146). As organizational knowledge increases, so does organizational capacity.

A robust effort to build and share knowledge provides two important benefits in an organization. First, knowledge equips team members for successful completion of tasks necessary to reach goals and fulfill the mission. Second, knowledge can help build relationships between team members, thus increasing the capacity of the organization. Zhang et al. (2019) put it this way:

> Knowledge sharing in teams, defined as interactive processes that team members share with each other their ideas, information, and advice relevant to the task, can promote creativity and innovation by facilitating knowledge flow and exchange between team members. In addition, team members also deepen their mutual understanding and social closeness in the process of knowledge sharing, thus further facilitating integrating and creating new ideas for novel and practical solutions. (p. 64, internal citations omitted)

A lack of knowledge can be an effective barrier to the success of any organization. This barrier can include not being aware of fiscal resources available, the skills within other team members, or exactly what tasks or problems need to be addressed. Access to knowledge can open many doors necessary to solve problems, complete tasks, and nurture the relationships necessary for organizational success.

TRAITS OF PEOPLED LEADERS

Leaders depend on people to solve problems, complete tasks, and ensure organizations progress toward the realization of their vision. Intelligence plays a role, but emotional intelligence plays a much bigger role because great leaders recognize and encourage quality relationships between themselves and others.

As indicated by its name, *Peopled Leadership* has as its foundational premise that people are central to the success of any organization. Strong relationships, built among the organization's people, form the solid ground necessary for strength, endurance, and success. One thing to remember is that there is no "I" in the word *team*. Together, all of the organization's people are stronger and know more than any individual member. This concept lies at the heart of the *Peopled Leadership* model. The *Peopled Leadership* model requires leaders that are selfless relationship builders who are humble, authentic, courageous, emotionally intelligent, empathetic, and committed to the organization and the individuals who comprise it.

In describing a peopled leader, we define humble as more than just avoiding the traps of being proud and arrogant. Humility requires the peopled leader to work from a servant mindset. Peopled leaders put others in the organization ahead of themselves. They focus on the professional and personal needs of the members of the organization. According to Greenleaf (2002), this type of leader has "the natural feeling that one wants to serve, to serve *first*" (emphasis in the original, p. 27). This type of leadership also requires authenticity. Greenleaf puts it this way: "Trust is first. Nothing will move until trust is firm" (p. 101).

Trust means the members of the organization have confidence that the head of the organization has the best interests of the organization and those who comprise it at heart. Organization heads, by virtue of their position, have different kinds of powers. French and Raven (1968, as cited by Hoy and Miskel, 2013) identified the following: reward power, coercive power, legitimate power, referent power, and expert power. Reward, coercive, and legitimate are organization powers, whereas referent and expert are personal powers. All can be used for the benefit of the organization. Likewise, all can be used to the detriment of the organization. Authentic leaders build confidence in internal and external stakeholders, and these powers need not be feared because they will be used to improve the organization and those who are a part of it.

Peopled leaders are also courageous leaders. *Merriam-Webster* (n.d.) defines courage as the "mental or moral strength to venture, persevere, and withstand danger, fear, or difficulty." Courage should be a thread that weaves itself throughout the work of a true leader. One key area of leadership that requires courage is making decisions. Ramsey (1999) asserts that "People expect their leaders to make decisions. That's what leadership is all about" (p. 11). Courageous leaders also have the conviction of what decisions need to or must be made unilaterally and what decisions are best decided by others in the organization. Courageous leaders also trust organization members with resources and knowledge so they are best equipped to help the organization progress toward realizing its vision.

Another characteristic of peopled leaders is the ability to be emotionally intelligent. Mayer and Salovey (1997) define emotional intelligence as "the ability to perceive emotions, to access and generate emotions so as to assist thought, to understand emotions and emotional thought, and to reflectively regulate emotions so as to promote emotional and intellectual growth" (p. 5). Peopled leaders constantly monitor the emotions of the individuals within the organization, the organization itself, and their own emotions. Emotional intelligence allows the peopled leader to be a better communicator through being a better listener. As Covey (1991) points out, "it is so important to listen primarily with our eyes and heart and secondarily with our ears. We must seek to understand the intent of the communication without prejudging or rejecting the content" (p. 116). Understanding the emotional condition of the people in the organization allows the leader to be sensitive, build trust with them, and be empathetic to their needs.

Closely related to emotional intelligence is the ability to have empathy for the members of the organization. Empathy is key to understanding how the members of the organization feel, to facilitating open, honest communication, and to using influence to the betterment of the organization (Covey, 1991). Finally, the peopled leader exhibits a commitment to the organization and to its individual members. Commitment means being loyal. It infers a promise to give one's best efforts each day. Commitment is necessary for documenting professional growth, producing needed change, and reaching personal and organizational goals (Covey, 1991).

Finally, peopled leaders practice gratitude. Being grateful reminds the leader of the value of all members of the organization and their importance to all phases of the operation. The practice of gratitude reinforces to members of the organization that they are valued, respected, needed, and appreciated. This is the fuel that ignites the burning desire to grow and achieve in the members of an organization.

Former President of the United States Dwight D. Eisenhower once said, "You don't lead by hitting people over the head. That's assault, not leadership." Peopled leaders know the real work of leadership is challenging each member of the group to face complex problems for which there are no simple, painless solutions—problems that require us to learn new ways of leading, being *Peopled Leaders*.

REFERENCES

Bartell, N., & Bartell K. (2016, July 23). *Radiant-leadership-model.* Bartell & Bartell. https://bartellbartell.com/home/attachment/radiant-leadership-model/

Bencsik, A., Jakubik, M., & Jubasz, T. (2020). The economic consequences of trust and distrust in knowledge-intensive organizations. *Journal of Competitiveness, 12*(3), 28–46. https://doi.org/10.7441/joc.2020.03.02

Covey, S. R. (1991). *Principle-centered leadership.* Simon and Schuster.

Dräger. (n.d.). *Dräger management.* Retrieved October 10, 2022, from https://www.draeger.com/en-us_us/Career/Leadership-Model

Farrell, M. (2016). Leadership reflections. *Journal of Library Administration, 56,* 444–452.

Fullan, M. (2008). *What's worth fighting for in the principalship* (2nd ed.). Teachers College Press.

Geier, M. T. (2016). Leadership in extreme contexts: Transformational leadership, performance beyond expectations? *Journal of Leadership & Organization Studies, 23*(3), 234–247.

Glickman, C., Gordon, S., & Ross-Gordon, J. (2018). *Supervision and instructional leadership: A developmental approach* (10th ed.). Pearson.

Greenleaf, R. (2002). *Servant leadership: A journey into the nature of legitimate power and greatness.* Paulist Press.

Heifetz, R., & Linsky, M. (2004). When leadership spells danger. *Educational Leadership, 61*(7), 33–37.

Hersey, P. (1984). *The situational leader.* Center for Leadership Studies.

Hoy, W. K., & Miskel, C. G. (2013). *Educational administration: Theory, research, and practice.* (9th ed.). McGraw-Hill.

Huntsman, D., & Greer, A. (2019). Antecedents of trust in leadership: A multilevel perspective in the Fire Service. *International Fire Service Journal of Leadership and Management, 13*(1), 19–33.

Jackson, R. (2021). *Stop leading, start building! Turn your school into a success story with the people and resources you already have.* Association for Supervision and Curriculum Development.

Kaplan, L., & Owings, W. (2015). *Introduction to the principalship: Theory to practice.* Routledge.

Kelly, J. (2018). *The crucible's gift: 5 lessons from authentic leaders who thrive in adversity.* Executives After Hours.

Levin, B., & Fullan, M. (2008). Learning about system renewal. *Educational Management Administration & Leadership, 36*(2), 289–303.

Lindell, J. M., Rhodes, A., & Watson, C. A. (2016). Preparing nurse leaders to innovate: Iowa's innovation seminar. *Journal of Nursing Education, 55*(2), 113–117.

Maxwell, J. C. (2019). *Leadershift: The 11 essential changes every leader must embrace.* HarperCollins Leadership.

Mayer, J. D., & Salovey, P. (1997). What is emotional intelligence? In P. Salovey & D. J. Sluyter (Eds.), *Emotional development and emotional intelligence: Educational implications* (pp. 3–31). Basic Books.

Merriam-Webster. (n.d.). Courage. In *Merriam-Webster.com dictionary.* Retrieved October 10, 2022, from https://www.merriam-webster.com/dictionary/courage

Mintzberg, H. (2004). *Managers Not MBAs.* Berrett-Koehler.

Nienaber, A., Hafeditz, M., & Romeike, P. D. (2015). Vulnerability and trust in leader-follower relationships. *Personnel Review, 44*(4), 567–591.

Paliszkiewicz, J., Goluchowski, J., & Koohang, A. (2015). Leadership, trust, and knowledge management in relation to organizational performance: Developing an instrument. *Online Journal of Applied Knowledge Management, 3*(2), 19–35.

Ramsey, R. D. (1999). *Lead, follow, or get out of the way: How to be a more effective leader in today's schools.* Corwin Press.

Right Management. (2014, January). *The flux report: Building a resilient workforce in the face of flux.* https://www.manpowergroup.co.uk/wp-content/uploads/2015/04/The-Flux-Report_whitepaper.pdf

Safer, L., Wilhite, R., & Mann, S. (2010). Applying adaptive leadership to sustain K-12 district initiatives and challenges. *International Journal of Educational Leadership Preparation, 5*(3). https://doi.org/https://cnx.org/contents/fYaCw4KM@2/Applying-Adaptive-Leadership-to-Sustain-K-12-District-Initiatives-and-Challenges

Tooley, M. (2021). *New research underscores need for new models of school leadership.* National Institute for Excellence in Teaching. https://www.niet.org/newsroom/show/blog/research-underscores-need-new-models-school-leadership

Whitehall, A. P., Bletscher, C. G., & Yost, D. M. (2021). Reflecting the wave, not the title: Increasing self-awareness and transparency of authentic leadership through online graduate student leadership programming. *Journal of Leadership Education, 20*(11), 114–127.

Wong, P., & Davey, D. (2007, July). *Best practices in servant leadership.* http://www.drpaulwong.com/wp-content/uploads/2013/09/wong-davey-2007-best-practices-in-servant-leadership.pdf

Zenger, J., & Folkman, J. (2002). *The extraordinary leader: Turning good managers into great leaders.* McGraw-Hill.

Zepeda, S. J., & Lanoue, P. D. (2021). *A leadership guide to navigating the unknown: New narratives amid COVID-19.* Routledge.

Zepeda, S. J., & Ponticell, J. A. (1998). At cross purposes: What do teachers need, want, and get from supervision? *Journal of Curriculum and Supervision, 14*(1) 68–87.

Zhang, W., Sun, S. L., Jiang, Y., & Zhang, W. (2019). Openness to experience and team creativity: Effects of knowledge sharing and transformational leadership. *Creativity Research Journal, 31*(1), 62–73.

Chapter 2

Peopled Leadership

People Oriented

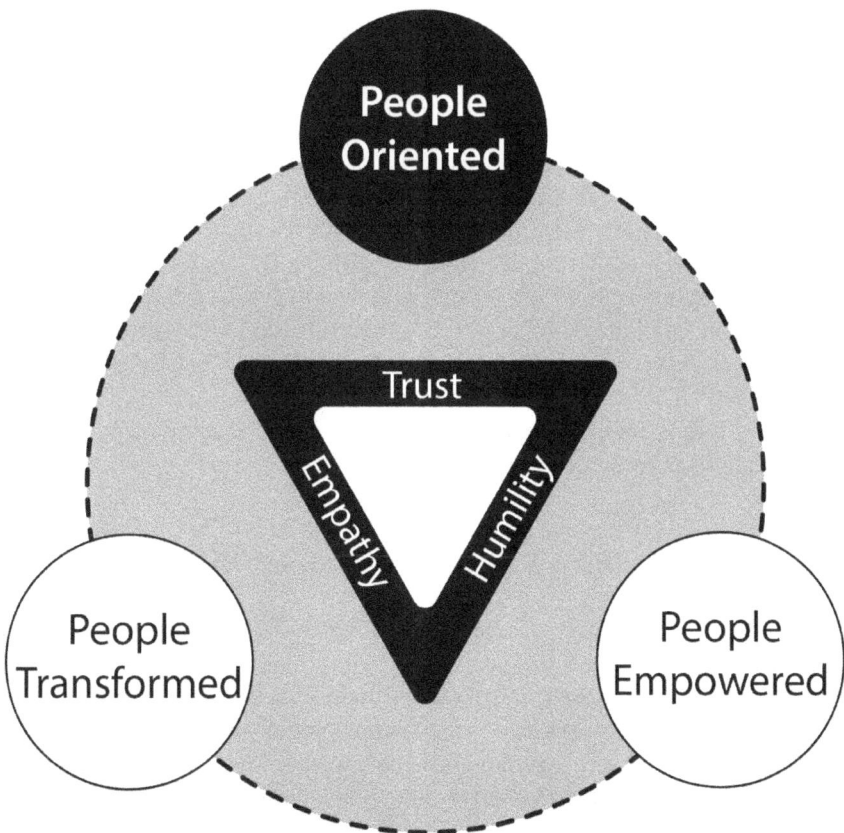

Fig. 2.1. *Peopled Leadership*: People Oriented. *Jack Ousey.*

Organizational structures are built around, engaged with, and designed to provide services to people. As such, organizational structures are social systems. In the pursuit of working with and shaping people, these are open social systems. As described by Hoy and Miskel (2013), "Social systems are peopled" (p. 24). Effective leaders in the 21st century must focus on more than outcomes and management of the organization; the best leaders focus on people. A people-oriented leader is one who builds trust and facilitates the creation of a compelling, collaborative vision that breathes life into the culture and climate of the organization. The people-oriented leader is a developer of people.

Peopled leaders understand the potential for achievement and greatness is inherent in all people. They put into practice Frei's maxim: "The most important decision we will make: how to remove barriers to people's unique capabilities" (Covey, 2022, p. 93). Maxwell (2019) described the essential nature of focusing on people: "My increased effort to first focus on others and to add value to them increased the energy of those I led—and it increased my energy while I was leading them" (p. 20). Further, quality leaders become aware of their people *in total*, not just as workers. This awareness is created through building trust and creating a shared vision for the organization.

A culture of trust in which people are valued and a common vision is created that identifies the shared values of the organization forms the foundation for a new model of leadership, *Peopled Leadership*. Until trust is established and shared values are identified, an organization cannot begin to achieve its desired outcomes, let alone realize its potential. This leadership model emerged from the belief that in any organization, it is individuals whose achievements combine to make possible the realization of desired outcomes. This chapter explores in depth the first phase of *Peopled Leadership*, People Oriented. The theoretical base is explored, key principles are identified, practical applications are discussed, and a case study with accompanying discussion questions is presented.

PHASE 1: PEOPLE-ORIENTED LEADERS

The first facet of *Peopled Leadership* is People Oriented. An open, social organization is made of people, serves people, and is served by people. Therefore, an effective leader must lead with the idea that people are the organization's most important asset. A key component in working with people is to establish working organizational relationships built on a firm foundation of trust and a compelling vision for the organization. Without trust, there is no leadership. Creating a vision for the organization involves two elements:

establishing expectations for the organization's culture and climate and identifying desired outcomes. A people-oriented leader and organization must be able to align culture and climate to the processes that will result in achieving desired outcomes.

In peopled-oriented leadership, the value of trust binds a compelling vision statement to the stakeholders in such a way that the organization becomes effective and efficient in pursuing its purpose and creating a picture of the future. Relationships established in trust can become effective in two-way communication and dynamic in collaborative efforts.

People-oriented leaders build relationships in an organization by establishing a compelling vision that supports clear communications and direction for the organization. Blanchard and Hodges (2008) describe organizational vision in terms of two parts based on the idea of leadership that puts people first: "a visionary role—setting the course and the destination" and "an implementation role—doing things right with a focus on serving" (p. 84). Developing a vision requires understanding what a vision should contain. Blanchard and Stoner (2003), describe three elements of vision: a statement of the organization's purpose, a picture of the organization's future, and an identification of the organization's values.

For people-oriented leaders, values are of greatest importance. A people-oriented leader builds effective, collaborative relationships with all organizational stakeholders. Often, organizational change is needed. It is a delicate balancing act to make the timely, needed changes the organization requires while taking time to build effective collaborative relationships. People-oriented leaders create a compelling vision by creating a culture that is aligned with the organization's values. This consistency, when paired with transparency, creates the conditions necessary to build trust. Mineo (2014) asserts, "When a leader speaks it is important to be able to have confidence in the honesty, truthfulness, and sincerity of the words. This is the essence of trust" (p. 1).

INTRODUCTION TO THE RESEARCH

The first phase of *Peopled Leadership*, people oriented, has its theoretical base in two bodies of leadership research: organizational values and trust. This research helps explain how leaders being people oriented can lead their organizations to create the conditions necessary to meet the organization's targeted outcomes. People-oriented leaders begin by establishing shared values and trust.

Values and Leadership

Values are central to the discussion of leadership (Freeman & Auster, 2011). According to Schein (2004), leadership and culture are two elements of the same entity, and the basic task of a leader is to create and maintain culture. Morrison et al. (2005) provide further support for the yoked nature of culture and values:

> Culture reveals the value base of schools; simply put, the rules of relationship management or the hidden social and emotional curriculum of school life. To assimilate into school culture requires the assimilation of school values. Conversely, the challenge of school culture requires the challenge of school values. (p. 340)

Creating a positive culture begins with the identification of values. Values and leadership are also inextricably linked. Best practices indicate the central importance of values and the need to recognize both individual and organizational values. Effective leaders treat organizational members as "rights holders" who are "creating value in an environmentally sustainable way" and are "becoming good citizens in a civil society" (Freeman & Auster, 2011, p. 15). Further, identification and adherence to shared values help create authenticity for the leader.

Values are a key component to leadership (Baloglu, 2012). They provide guidance (Davis, 2011); assist with problem solving (Kouzes & Posner, 1993); and help create and when necessary, restore relationships (Morrison et al., 2005). Values are also key to achieving the ultimate goal of transforming the organization. Transformation targets values and begins with leadership. Lee (2004) explains:

> Transformational process will change mind-sets, target values and build a culture which can truly support new strategies and organisational aspirations. However it can only be driven by passionate and persistent leadership at the top. Therefore, transformational change begins with transforming the mind-sets of managers. (p. 39)

As the organization identifies the values it shares and by which it wishes to be defined, the issue of authenticity may be addressed.

Vision-driven improvement that is data informed appears to be the newest wave in leadership reform. However, all organizations should be vision driven. A compelling vision is not something that easily fits on a company letterhead or Friday casual T-shirt. Blanchard and Hodges (2008) describe a compelling vision statement as having three parts. First, a compelling vision tells the organization and the public what business you are in, what you do, and what you produce. A compelling vision also gives a vision of what you think the future looks like for the people affected by your organization.

Finally, a compelling vision shares the common guiding values of the organization. In the case of a people-oriented organization, one of the guiding values must be trust. Peopled leaders are authentic. Authenticity is the ability to be consistent with who one professes to be. To be authentic requires a careful examination of oneself. Freeman and Auster (2011) refer to this examination as looking into the "poet self" or "the intersection of our values, our past, our set of connections to others, and our aspirations" (p. 20). Becoming authentic lays the foundation for building trust.

Trust

Covey (2018) begins *The Speed of Trust* with the following:

> There is one thing that is common to every individual, relationship, team, family, organization, nation, economy, and civilization throughout the world—one thing which, if removed, will destroy the most powerful government, the most successful business, the most thriving economy, the most influential leadership, the greatest friendship, the strongest character, the deepest love. On the other hand, if developed and leveraged, that one thing has the potential to created unparalleled success and prosperity in every dimension of life. Yet, it is the least understood, most neglected, and most underestimated possibility of our time. That one thing is trust. Trust impacts us 24/7, 365 days a year. (p. 1)

The cornerstone for becoming people oriented is trust. Trust is a multifaceted construction that has been defined in a myriad of ways. Paliszkiewicz (2011) adds the dimension of communication to the definition of trust:

> Trust in organizations involves employees' willingness to be vulnerable to their organization's actions. This willingness can be rendered only when an organization clearly communicates its actions to its employees through informal and formal networks. An important source of information is the employee's immediate social environment, which largely comprises coworkers. (p. 319)

Mayer et al. (1995) define trust as "the willingness of a party to be vulnerable to the actions of another party based on the expectation that the other will perform a particular action important to the trustor, irrespective of the ability to monitor or control that other party" (p. 712). Gambetta (1988) defined trust in terms of relationships, believing that trust implies a leader's behaviors are constructive and not detrimental to any person.

Sztompka (1999) defines trust based on the expectations held about other people. Trust means other people act in ways that contribute to the well-being of others and involves two components: beliefs and commitments. Members of the organization believe in the consistency and transparency of the leader and are willing to commit to the vision of the organization. Further, trust involves "acting in uncertain and uncontrollable conditions . . . tak[ing] risks, gambl[ing]. . . . trust is a bet about the future contingent actions of others" (p. 25). The leader's responsibility is to create a culture that helps elevate the probability of success in the risk-taking and gambling characteristic of healthy organizations.

While vulnerability is not considered a human value, it is a necessary condition for trust to be present. Vulnerability lies at the very core of trust, and leaders need to be able to understand the difference between "the willingness to be vulnerable and actual vulnerability" (Nienaber et al., 2015, p. 571). Chambers (2006) believes vulnerability occurs in response to two sources: external threats and a lack of internal coping mechanisms:

> Vulnerability has . . . two sides: an external side of risks, shocks, and stress to which an individual . . . is subject; and an internal side which is defenselessness, meaning a lack of means to cope without damaging loss. (p. 33)

Moving the organization to the point where members are comfortable and willing to be vulnerable and take risks is difficult but necessary for the peopled leader. Otherwise, needed relationships between leaders and organization members or among organization members cannot be developed.

Building trust in an organization is a desirable as well as a challenging goal (Zhang et al., 2008); it is necessary for peopled leaders. Three reasons that make trust building difficult have been identified in the empirical literature. First, trust building requires two individuals that interactively learn about each other's trustworthiness. Second, trust building is dependent on positive feedback, but is a gradual, incremental process that is reinforced by previous trusting behaviors and positive experiences. Third, there is no guarantee trust will be honored (Paliszkiewicz, 2011). These factors explain the complexity of trust building.

To more fully understand the complexity of trust building in organizations, it is helpful to review Covey's (2018) "five waves" of trust:

> *Self-trust*: The confidence a leader has to "set and achieve goals, to keep commitments, to walk our talk, and also our ability to inspire others."

> *Relationship trust*: Consistent behaviors that allow leaders to build "trust accounts" with individuals in the organization.

> *Organizational trust*: Establishing and maintaining alignment of purpose and actions that promote trust throughout the organization.

Market trust: Creating and maintaining a reputation that allows external stakeholders to have confidence in engaging with the organization. Strong market trust enhances both the organization's and the leader's reputation.

Societal trust: The organization makes a contribution to society as a whole. (pp. 32–35)

The first three of Covey's waves of trust are particularly relevant to the peopled-oriented phase of the *Peopled Leadership* model.

The peopled leader begins by working on self-trust, being a person of consistency, transparency, and compassion. These characteristics help establish the leader's trustworthiness. After a leader produces a track record of trustworthiness, relationships with organization members can be developed. Relationship trust can now begin to be developed. Relationship trust refers to trust within the organization and is based on the concept of consistent behavior by leaders and by members. Relationship trust makes possible the kind of culture that allows the organization to create and refine its vision and to achieve its basic goals. Organizational trust allows members to trust the organization as a whole. Leaders facilitate and nurture structures and systems that are aligned with the organization's vision and goals. Organizational trust fosters behaviors that help the organization grow and protect it from behaviors that are toxic and would prevent desired outcomes from being reached (Covey, 2018).

Building trust within and across an organization requires a leader that demonstrates strong personal trustworthiness. Peopled leaders develop a variety of tools for building trust. The empirical literature on trust reveals three main tools or behaviors are key to building trust: consistency, transparency, and accountability. Peopled leaders are consistent in their behaviors, especially in the keeping of commitments to the organization (Covey, 2018). This includes all sources of support and resources needed for individuals in the organization to carry out their tasks. This especially includes the leader's time.

Trustworthiness also requires transparency. As much information as possible is shared in a timely fashion with all concerned members of the organization. Within an organization, information is a form of power (Raven, 2008). Raven defines information power as the ability of a leader to provide necessary instruction about the nature and requirements of a task and how this exchange of information promotes the timely completion of the task. According to Raven (2008), when a leader provides this information in a trusting environment, the organization member does not necessarily perceive the leader as the agent of the changed behavior brought about by the information. Within the *Peopled Leadership* model, information power creates shared knowledge and the synergy and culture necessary for individual and organizational success. Transparency with information is key to building and maintaining trust (Farrell, 2016). As Justice Louis Brandeis wrote in a 1913 *Harper's Weekly* article, "Sunlight is said to be the best of disinfectants."

Accountability is a requirement for trust. Practicing accountability begins with the leader. Holding oneself accountable builds trustworthiness. Accountability also helps to clarify expectations, increases organization members' responsiveness to tasks to be completed, and builds a sense in members that they are respected and valued (Covey, 2018). In addition, accountability empowers members of the organization to emerge as leaders themselves through becoming servant leaders to their colleagues (Norris et al., 2017).

BASIC PRINCIPLES OF
PEOPLE-ORIENTED LEADERSHIP

The first phase of the *Peopled Leadership* model is people oriented, which has two separate but related meanings. First, oriented indicates a beginning. The leaders are getting to know the members of the organization and getting to know themselves better as well. In particular, this exploration should result in the identification of what is important to the leaders and members of the organization. These priorities will help determine the values of the organization. The second, related meaning is that of focus. The most important resource of any organization is its people. Therefore, effective leaders keep their primary focus on their people, showing care and support, providing resources, and giving guidance where needed and when requested. This people-oriented work can only be done in an atmosphere of trust. Therefore, the first priority of leadership is building trust. Thus, the guiding principles of the people-oriented phase of the model are (1) identifying and agreeing on values, (2) building trust within oneself, and (3) building trust with the members of the organization.

Identifying and Agreeing on Organizational Values

Organizational values are guiding principles that govern how members of an organization interact with one another and external stakeholders. Values generally can be classified as either general or organizationally specific. General values reflect how most people want to be treated by others. These values include being respected, valued, and supported in terms of resources and emotionally during times of stress. Examples of organizationally specific values would include casual dress and greetings in a retail establishment;

sportsmanship for an athletic team; or personal courage when facing fear, danger, or adversity for the armed services.

Identifying the values needed by the organization begins with introspection by the leader. Whether planned or not, the values of the leader tend to be reflected in the organization. As the leader, what principles will guide your interactions with organization members and stakeholders? What principles do you want to see at work when you observe interactions between members and/or stakeholders? Once the leader has identified the "critical few" values, the next step is to involve organization members in completing the task. It is important that organizational values belong to the organization, not just the leader. This requires focused time together as a team. While face-to-face meetings have advantages, remote meeting technology should be a tool at the disposal of every 21st-century leader.

Ask your people what they value. Discover what will improve their experience working for your organization. Find out what principles they will expect you to uphold. Then, negotiate to finalize a set of values that will govern the practices of your organization. A people-oriented leader monitors staff meetings, email communications, and personal interactions to ensure consistent adherence to the agreed-upon values. Interactions that are not consistent with those values are addressed either informally or in the case of a pattern of disregard, formally with a follow-up strategy as needed. Adherence to agreed-upon values is often the difference between a collaborative, problem-solving, goal-reaching organization where people thrive and a dysfunctional organization that loses people and demoralizes those that remain.

A few years ago, the Department of Educational Instruction and Leadership at Southeastern Oklahoma State University decided it needed a set of agreed-on values for its operations. The chair provided one "nonnegotiable" value: department members would "respect, value, and care for" one another. From this basis, the department identified other needed values, such as being our authentic selves, working collaboratively, and being supportive and responsive to each other's needs. People's needs exist on many levels: physical, mental, emotional, social, and spiritual. The best leaders (think people-oriented leaders) are sensitive to and serve the needs of organization members on all of these levels. To be this kind of leader, one must learn as much as possible about those in the organization. This skill is addressed in the last two principles of people-oriented leaders: building trust within oneself and building trust with the members of the organization.

Establishing and Maintaining Self- and Relationship Trust

Trust is essential to effective leadership; without trust, one cannot lead. As Covey (2018) points out, trust "is the least understood, most neglected, and most underestimated possibility of our time" and "trust impacts us 24/7, 365 days a year" (p. 1). Therefore, the number one job of the leader, every single day, is building and maintaining trust within the organization. Trust is prerequisite to being able to instill an organization's values, meet members' needs, and achieve any desired outcome. Building trust begins within the leader.

Returning to Covey's (2018) five waves of trust, to be a people-oriented leader, one must focus first on developing self-trust, or the confidence that one can lead. This involves the commitment to facilitate the establishment of organizational values and then to consistently model them through one's behavior. As the leader becomes confident in the development of self-trust, the development of relationship trust can begin. The leader begins building trust with each member of the organization by learning more about each member and finding ways to meet the needs of each one. Covey (2018) refers to this process as building "trust accounts." Finally, the leader can move from building trust with individual organization members to building trust between organization members. This is organization trust (Covey, 2018). When organization trust becomes a cultural norm, collaboration also becomes the norm, and the organization has truly become a team.

To begin, the leader must be consistent. Every interaction with every organization member is important. As consistency develops, the next step of developing trust can occur. Practices such as humility and gratitude can form a firm foundation for creating the consistency necessary for people-oriented leaders. Leading with humility communicates that each organization member is also a leader and the leader is also an organization member. Gratitude reinforces that each organization member is respected and valued as persons and as professionals with skills and abilities important to the organization. Humility and gratitude as leadership skills are discussed in more detail later in this book.

Trust requires the ability to make oneself vulnerable, and this also begins with the leader. Peopled leaders share themselves with their team members, their likes and dislikes, hobbies, and other personal information that is appropriate for the workplace and will allow other team members to get to know them better. This process begins slowly, and as consistency builds and trust begins to form, sharing oneself not only occurs with greater frequency; sharing will also begin to occur in greater depth. This idea of sharing is critical for leaders to become people-oriented leaders. The more a leader knows about the members of the organization, the better the leader is positioned to meet their needs.

As the leader becomes more vulnerable and open to other members of the organization, others in the organization will follow suit. This development in the organization does not happen overnight, nor does it occur in each organizational member simultaneously. It is a process that requires daily nurturing amid an understanding that organization members experience and progress through the process at their own pace. Two indispensable skills for the leader facilitating this process are listening and observing. Verbal and nonverbal cues provide information for the leader about organizational members' readiness to move forward in becoming more open and thus more toward being vulnerable. Examples of potentially important observations around the workplace include seeing new combinations of workers engaged together in organizational tasks, more collegial communications, and even laughter.

One truism every leader must understand is that in every life, "stuff" happens. Illness, bereavement, job loss, and natural disasters are just some of the "stuff" than can derail life, not to mention job performance. It is in these moments that people-oriented leaders can make the deepest impact on the lives of organization members as well as the organization itself. When organizational members receive a potentially devastating diagnosis, helping them adjust their workload to accommodate needed treatment, rest, and recuperation is the job of the people-oriented leader. In addition to serving the needs of the organization members, the leaders are also continuing to build trust, with the affected members and others as well. Further, the cultivating of another by-product of trust, collaboration, leads to other team members "picking up the slack" to help a colleague and to keep the organization moving toward its desired outcomes.

People-Oriented Leaders, Building Trust, and Difficult Organization Members

In any organization, there is always the possibility of a member that for a variety of reasons, may be reluctant to agree to or comply with values agreed upon by the others. A well-constructed, compelling vision statement can help keep members of the organization focused on the values and goals of the organization. While the severity and the nature of the issues may make it necessary to develop a specific plan to deal with that employee, it is always preferable to find informal ways to bring about compliance. People-oriented leaders focus on building relationships. This process, discussed elsewhere in this book, involves careful listening, providing guidance, and establishing agreement on future behaviors. Meet privately with the reluctant employee to identify the nature and the source of the issues. See if a mutually agreeable solution can be reached. Formulate a plan for informal data gathering to see if the agreed-upon practices are being used. Keep notes to track progress or the lack of it.

Unfortunately, some reluctant or uncompliant employees will not change their ways to become more complaint with organizational values. If progress toward compliance cannot be made, it may be necessary to part ways. The former superintendent of a suburban school district in a major metropolitan area used a school bus analogy to demonstrate the purpose of a vision statement for her organization. When addressing the issues of reluctant or marginal employees, she said, "Our school district is like a school bus and the vision tells us where we are going. Sometimes you have to explain to someone, 'this is the way we are going. If you do not want to go with us, maybe you need to get off this bus.'" To keep the "bus" clean and moving toward the desired organizational outcomes, separation may be necessary.

Application to Problems of Practice for 21st-Century Leaders

One of the problems with peopled organizations is that the organization cannot be completely controlled or guided by policy. There will be situations, circumstances, and even people who are outliers; they do not fit nicely into the "policy box." Recent events have brought forth new challenges for leaders of various organizations. A worldwide pandemic, increased food insecurity, and rampant inflation have created new issues related to employee physical, mental, and emotional health. According to Mental Health America (2020), 47 million adult Americans were reported with some type of mental illness in 2021, a number that had held steady for a decade (Substance Abuse and Mental Health Services Administration, 2014). In one year, the number of Americans reported with some type of mental illness rose sharply to 50 million (Mental Health America, 2021).

The increasing incidence of mental health issues presents a difficult challenge for leaders and serves to underscore the need for leaders to be people oriented. Clean, clear communication is difficult in 21st-century workplaces. Never before has there been so much information through which the average person must sift each day. According to Chaffey (2022), there are 4.7 billion social media users in the world, representing 59% of the world's population. Over the past year, 227 million new users have begun using social media, for an average of 7 new users every second. Managing this onslaught of new information requires new training, knowledge, and skills (Pekkala & van Zoonen, 2021). Careful monitoring of organization members and having resources for support and treatment when needed are critical to successful leadership in the 21st century.

The pandemic of 2020 combined with the emergence of new and enhanced virtual meeting platforms changed the perceptions and reality of what defines the workplace. At the height of the pandemic, 35.4% of the workforce worked remotely (U.S. Bureau of Labor, 2022). Although improving pandemic conditions have led to a steep decrease in the number of teleworkers, the practice remains popular. As of 2021, 26.7% of Americans work remotely, and that number is expected to increase over the next several years (Flynn, 2022). The most commonly cited reasons for remote work include better work–life balance, less time spent in traffic, and more control of the expenditure of time (Pordelan et al., 2022).

The leader's challenge to monitor the well-being of organization members is enhanced due to the increase in telework. Regular, professional communication is critical to monitoring the well-being and productivity of teleworking organization members. The challenges of leading teleworking team members also demands high levels of trust. Check-in emails and periodic virtual meetings are effective tools for staying in touch with remote organization members. However, it is important that these meetings not be seen as the leader checking up on the member in a negative sense. They need to be seen as trust building communications that support team building and goal achievement.

How the Model Helps Bridge the Gap Between Relevant Research and Practice

Leadership duties can be distracting. A compelling vision can keep the leader focused on the purpose for the organization. The leader and to some extent, the leadership team (where one exists) establish the structure and practice or climate of the organization. By including organizational values in the vision statement, the leader establishes the base by which people will be treated.

CASE STUDY

A new principal (with six years of teaching experience) of a small, rural middle school is trying to focus on instructional time while still allowing for fun student activities. The practice has been to have a pep rally for one home football game. The middle school cheerleaders perform at this pep rally and at the high school homecoming pep rally. While meeting with the middle school cheerleading coach (also new this year), the coach and principal have found themselves in a disagreement about how many pep rallies to schedule.

Several days later, after a particularly grueling day for the principal, the middle school cheerleaders line up across the street to block the principal's car as he is leaving campus. They and their new coach demand to have a pep rally for every football game. The principal explains that he believes increasing the number of pep rallies is not feasible due to required schedule changes for each day with loss of learning time. The following day, several parents post memes and messages on social media attacking your decision. A day later, the cheerleading coach shares some of the memes on her social media accounts.

The next morning, you meet with the cheerleading coach, which results in an informal warning about her social media usage and her incitement of parents against you. Later that day, you are called to the superintendent's office for a meeting. The superintendent has received emails and phone calls from several parents complaining about the pep rally situation and your dealings with the coach. Afterward, privately, the superintendent asks if the number of pep rallies versus 30 minutes of instructional time per week is really a sword worth falling on.

DISCUSSION QUESTIONS

1. What did the principal do correctly in the scenario? What about the superintendent?
2. What evidence did you find of vulnerability?
3. Assess the trust level between the principal and coach.
4. Assess the trust level between the principal and superintendent.
5. How would you assess the values of the middle school?
6. How would you assess the values of the district?
7. Are the two sets of values consistent?

REFERENCES

Baloglu, N. (2012). Relations between value-based leadership and distributed leadership: A casual research on school principals' behaviors. *Educational Sciences, Theory and Practice, 12*(2), 1375–1378.

Blanchard, K., & Hodges, P. (2008). *Lead like Jesus.* Thomas Nelson.

Blanchard, K., & Stoner, J. (2003). *Full steam ahead: The power of vision.* Berrett-Kohler.

Chaffey, D. (2022, August 22). *Global social media statistics research summary 2022.* Smart Insights. https://www.smartinsights.com/social-media-marketing/social-media-strategy/new-global-social-media-research/

Chambers, R. (2006). Vulnerability, coping and policy. *IDS Bulletin, 37*(4), 33–40. https://doi.org/10.1111/j.1759-5436.2006.tb00284.x

Covey, S. M. R. (2018). *The speed of trust: The one thing that changes everything.* Free Press.

Covey, S. M. R. (2022). *Trust & inspire: How truly great leaders unleash greatness in others.* Simon & Schuster.

Davis, J. W. (2011). *Sacred leadership: Leading for the greatest good.* Davis Group, Ltd. http://www.davisgroupltd.net/?/page_id=10

Farrell, M. (2016). Leadership reflections. *Journal of Library Administration, 56*(3), 444–452.

Flynn, J. (2022). *Remote work statistics [2022]: Facts, trends and projections.* Zippia. https://www.zippia.com/advice/remote-work-statistics/

Freeman, R. E., & Auster, E. R. (2011). Values, authenticity, and responsible leadership. *Journal of Business Ethics, 98*(1), 15–23.

Gambetta, D. (1988). Can we trust trust? In D. Gambetta (Ed.), *Trust: Making and breaking cooperative relations* (pp. 213–237). Basil Blackwell.

Hoy, W. K., & Miskel, C. G. (2013). *Educational administration: Theory, research, and practice* (9th ed.). McGraw-Hill.

Kouzes, J. M., & Posner, B. Z. (1993). *Credibility: How leadership gain and lose it, why people demand it.* Jossey-Bass.

Lee, T. (2004). Cultural change agent: Leading transformational change. In C. Barker and R. Coy (Eds.), *The power of culture: Driving today's organisation.* McGraw-Hill.

Maxwell, J. C. (2019). *Leadershift: The 11 essential changes every leader must embrace.* HarperCollins Leadership.

Mayer, R. C., Davis, J. H., & Schoorman, F. D. (1995). An integrative model of organizational trust. *The Academy of Management Review, 20*(3), 709–734.

Mental Health America. (2020, October 20). *2021 State of mental health in America.* https://www.mhanational.org/research-reports/2021-state-mental-health-america

Mental Health America. (2021, October 19). *2022 State of mental health in America.* https://www.mhanational.org/research-reports/2022-state-mental-health-america-report

Mineo, D. L. (2014). The importance of trust in leadership. *Research Management Review, 20*(1), 1–6.

Morrison, B., Blood, P., & Thorsborne, M. (2005). Practicing restorative justice in school communities: The challenge of culture change. *Public Organization Review, 5*(2), 335–357.

Nienaber, A., Hofeditz, M., & Romelke, P. D. (2015). Vulnerability and trust in leader-follower relationships. *Personnel Review, 44*(4), 567–591.

Norris, S., Sitton, S., & Baker, M. (2017). Mentorship through the lens of servant leadership: The importance of accountability and empowerment. *North American Colleges and Teachers of Agriculture, 61*(1), 21–26.

Paliszkiewicz, J. O. (2011). Trust management: Literature review. *Management, 6*(4), 315–331.

Pekkala, K., & van Zoonen, W. (2021). Work-related social media use: The mediating role of social media communication self-efficacy. *European Management Journal, 40*(1), 67–76.

Pordelan, N., Hosseinian, S., Heydari, H., Khalijian, S., & Khorrami, M. (2022). Consequences of teleworking using the internet among married working women:

Educational careers investigation. *Education and Information Technologies*, *27*(3), 4277–4299.

Raven, B. H. (2008). The bases of power/interaction model of interpersonal influence. *Analysis of Social Issues and Public Policy*, *8*(1), 1–22.

Schein, E. H. (2004). *Organizational culture and leadership* (3rd ed.). Jossey-Bass.

Substance Abuse and Mental Health Services Administration. (2014, October 10). *Results from the 2012 National Survey on Drug Use and Health: Mental health findings.* U.S. Department of Health and Human Services. https://www.samhsa.gov/data/report/results-2012-national-survey-drug-use-and-health-mental-health-findings

Sztompka, P. (1999). *Trust: A sociological theory.* Cambridge University Press.

U.S. Bureau of Labor. (2022, May 11). *TED: The economics daily: 7.7 Percent of workers teleworked due to COVID-19 in April 2022.* https://www.bls.gov/opub/ted/2022/7-7-percent-of-workers-teleworked-due-to-covid-19-in-april-2022.htm

Zhang, A. Y., Tsui, A. S., Song, L. J., Chaoping, L., & Jia, L. (2008). How do I trust thee? *Human Resource Management*, *47*(1), 111–132.

Chapter 3

Peopled Leadership

People Empowered

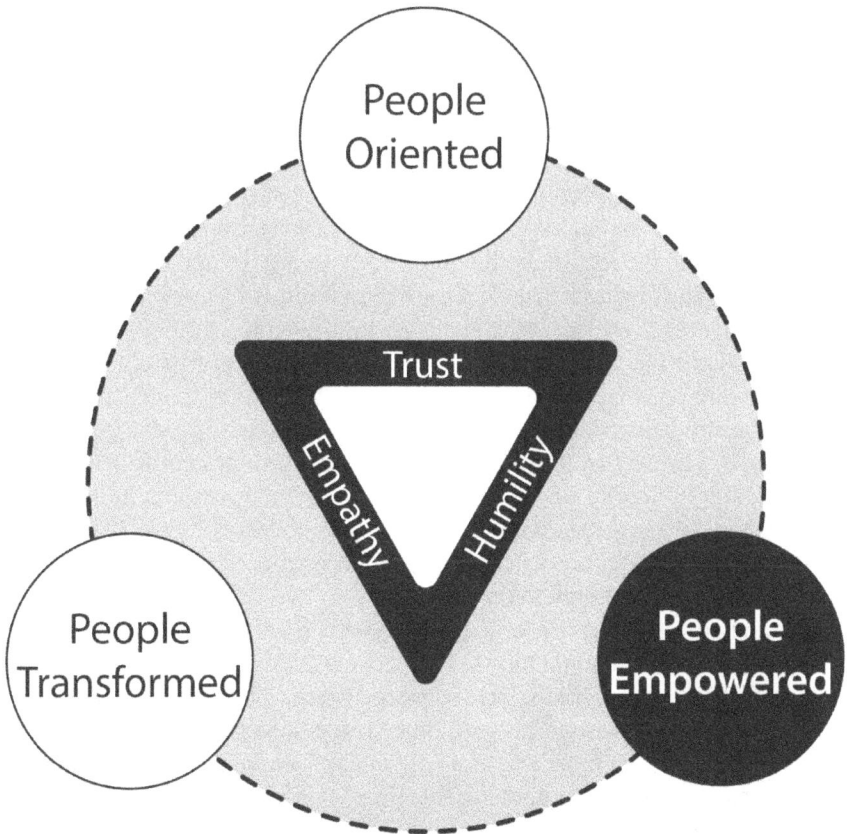

Fig. 3.1. *Peopled Leadership*: People Empowered. *Jack Ousey.*

Leadership has evolved in unprecedented ways over the last several years. Pandemics, legislated accountability, controversial policy initiatives, employee shortages, challenging funding systems, trauma responsiveness needed to support those served by organizations, language barriers, influx of new technology, and generational nuances and expectations of employees lie at the heart of just some of the challenges leaders face today. For organizations to be successful, leaders must act on the fact that it does take the expertise of everyone. Therefore, today's leaders, perhaps more than ever, need to create *more leaders* (Wiseman, 2017) to solve complex problems and ensure opportunity for the organization to be successful.

Such opportunities that allow for true collaborative leadership require vulnerability and the mutual trust established and nurtured through the people-oriented phase of the *Peopled Leadership* model. Leaders must trust in the ability, heart, intentions, and willingness of others to authentically engage in the demanding work associated with leadership. Those willing to work alongside leaders and undertake leadership activities must trust their leaders to allow for pushback, risk-taking, and transparency.

To lead with humility, provide resources equitably, create a culture of autonomy, and empower others to collaboratively engage and help lead an organization are not routine or easy tasks. Leaders who practice humility allow others a voice and an opportunity to shine while they are willing to fade into the background as their members grow as professionals. Such leaders know they cannot "go it alone" if their organization is to succeed. Frostenson (2016) proposes the idea that "humility involves joy in other people's success" (p. 91) and suggests that "Virtues like humility are among the phenomena at a personal level that bring about positive outcomes" (p. 95).

Leaders have the ultimate responsibility to ensure impactful opportunities to help ensure organizational success. To share the leadership of an organization, while still being fully responsible for its success, is a paradox. Sebastian et al. (2016) believe that leaders play a valuable role in promoting leadership by delegating authority and empowering others "in ways that allow them influence in key organizational decisions and processes" (p. 69). Leaders must also create a culture where organization members are seen as professionals and have autonomy to do the work.

Additionally, leaders are charged with providing the necessary resources so that members of the community can effectively impact those they serve and help fulfill the vision and mission of the organization. The strategic allocation and management of resources (e.g., time, space, materials, and budget) has a profound impact on members of an organizational community, resulting in empowerment and transformation. Therefore, it is vital that those outside of a leadership role have input in discussions of resource allocation.

PHASE 2: PEOPLE-EMPOWERED LEADERSHIP

The second phase of *Peopled Leadership* is People Empowered. Open systems are people-centered organizations; therefore, all members of the organization are the focus of the leader. People-empowered leaders regard organization members as mission critical and invest in creating a culture that uplifts and celebrates members and allows members to be an active part of the success of the organization. A people-empowered leader acts with humility, empowers organization members, allows and encourages professional independence, and protects and provides necessary resources to support all members of the organization.

People-empowered leaders think deeply about how to exercise authority without being authoritative. They believe in and act with the knowledge that there are many leaders in an organization, and such leaders harness the gifts, abilities, and expertise of all members. Humility is the linchpin for how people-empowered leaders approach leadership. They have a deeply held belief that they are learners as well as leaders and can learn from others. They know that the organization's success is dependent on all members, not just those in positions of authority or formal leadership roles. They are transparent about their struggles and mistakes, modeling that everyone needs help and support. Humility drives how such leaders engage in daily management and leadership and how they act and treat others, and they share the lens by which they make decisions and place value on the collective voice of the organization.

INTRODUCTION TO THE RESEARCH

The second phase of *Peopled Leadership*, people empowered, is grounded in several research areas: humility, empowerment and autonomy, and resources. This body of research is designed to provide a path for people-empowered leaders to best support the people of the organization and those served by the organization to achieve organizational success.

Humility

Kouzes and Posner (2012) remind us that "A grand dream doesn't become a significant reality through the actions of a single person. It requires team effort. It requires solid trust and relationships" (p. 21) and allowing others to have a "seat at the table" and knowing that "sharing the table" is vital for the success of the organization and is a trait of a humble leader. Kouzes and

Posner (2012) assert that exceptional leaders approach leadership and their role with deep humility, noting

> Humility is the antidote for hubris. You can avoid excessive pride only when you recognize that you are human and need the help of others. Exemplary leaders know that you can't do it alone and they act accordingly. They lack the pride and pretense displayed by many leaders who succeeded in the short term but leave behind a weak organization that fails to remain viable after their departure. Instead, with self-effacing humor, deep listening to those around them, and generous and sincere credit to others, humble leaders realize higher and higher levels of performance. (p. 341)

In short, there is a true acknowledgment that with humility, leaders can overcome the paradox of leadership, which resides in power.

By being humble, leaders gain influence and power by giving those very aspects of leadership to others. Owens et al. (2013) define humility as "an interpersonal characteristic that emerges in social contexts that connotes (a) a manifested willingness to view oneself accurately, (b) a displayed appreciation of others' strengths and contributions, and (c) teachability" (p. 1518). They assert that humility is "one of the core organizational virtues that are proposed to provide the moral foundation of organizational environments" (p. 1517). Owens et al. (2013) contend that

> Humility has been included as one of the core "organizational virtues" that are proposed to provide the moral foundation of organizational environments. Theorists have proposed that humility is becoming more critical for leaders who direct their organizations in increasingly dynamic and turbulent environments . . . for instance, that the increasing "unpredictability and unknowability" organizations face will require leaders of the 21st century to have "more humility and less hubris." (p. 1517)

They further argue that "Given its relational nature, expressed humility will be especially relevant in contexts that entail frequent interactions with people and where the content of the interactions is to exchange information, feedback, and criticism" (p. 1519).

Chiu and Hung (2020) suggest that when leaders act with humility, they admit their mistakes and limitations and they do not pretend to know everything. Humble leaders know their people are the most valuable resource, and they "are as dependent on their followers as the followers are on them" (p. 403). They further contend that leader humility fosters trustworthiness and helps organizations achieve goals. Chiu and Hung (2020) found:

While leaders constantly encounter traditional challenges regarding the survival of their enterprises, in contemporary times, they are also challenged regarding their integrity and morality; as heroic and charismatic beliefs in leadership are less emphasized, the authentic, ethical, and spiritual aspects of leaders' self-awareness are emerging. In retrospect, leaders need to pursue their inner self and the essence of leadership; exploring the concept of humility may somewhat illuminate the maze of modern leadership. (p. 415)

Dubrin (2007) argues that an important "understanding of leadership is that it is a long-term relationship, or partnership, between leaders and group members" (p. 3). He proposes that when leaders are focused on partnerships and relationships, shared trust is developed, and all parties gain an optimistic view of their organizational members. Forming partnerships between leaders and those being led is dependent on humility. Such leaders are willing to let others take the credit, acknowledge that they cannot do the work alone, and develop a culture of collective efficacy.

Empowerment and Autonomy

Hoy and Miskel (2013) define empowerment as the way leaders "share power and help others use it in constructive ways to make decisions affecting themselves and their work" (p. 240). When leaders empower those they lead, their organizations can experience sustained success. When people are empowered, they perform at higher levels and are more connected to the organization. According to Kouzes and Posner (2012):

In the best organizations, everyone, regardless of title or position, is encouraged to act like a leader. That's because in these places, people don't just believe that everyone can make a difference, they act in ways to develop and grow other people's talents, including their leadership capabilities. (p. 14)

Urban (2019) argues that "Understanding and leveraging the ability to actively engage and embrace empowerment can build high-performing teams—if done correctly." Suda (2013) offers thoughts about the need for leaders to create relationships and develop organization members who have the capacity to lead. Suda contends that leadership is part of a supportive bond where leaders depend on others and members of the organization depend on leaders (para. 2). Suda further defines the concept of leadership as primarily an influencing role and notes the nature of relationships involving shared commitment and collaborative leadership "involve reciprocity, the mutual exchange of influence" (para. 5).

Leithwood and Mascall (2008) argue that the concept of leadership around a solitary heroic leader, "the great [one]," has shifted to include collaborative leadership relationships (p. 529). Kaplan and Owings (2015) contend that "With strategic planning, managerial, instructional, political, human resources, and symbolic roles to play [leaders] cannot do everything that needs to be done by themselves" (p. 216). Sebastian et al. (2016) assert that leaders "work through other leaders" to develop supports and processes by delegating authority empowering others and involving organization members and others in setting "direction and organizing their daily operations" (p. 72).

Urban (2019) suggests that leaders are sometimes mistaken about what empowerment actually is and thus provides examples of these mistaken views. Urban explains that empowerment is not simply offering a suggestion box for the purpose of idea gathering, providing team-building exercises, and touting an open-door policy and notes these activities are supportive of a healthy culture but they do not in and of themselves create empowered people. Empowerment is more expansive, has more depth, and suggests "leadership must be highly engaged in building an environment that encourages sharing, collaboration, challenging the status quo, and progressive improvement" (para. 2–6). Urban (2019) provides five leadership activities that support empowerment of followers: identifying and leveraging the strengths of all members; regularly training and developing the capacity of others; modeling and supporting continuous improvement; creating an environment where people can learn from their experiences in a "fail forward," not fear of failure culture; and letting organization members take appropriate risks.

When leaders focus on and are committed to empowering others, those leaders unleash talent, commitment, and capacity. Wiseman (2017) maintains that "Multipliers are leaders who look beyond their own genius and focus their energy on extracting and extending the genius of others" (p. 11). Wiseman finds that such leaders create "genius makers" who multiply an organization's collective ability and impact (p. 10). When such leaders, multipliers, empower others, they attract capability, intelligence, and commitment.

Autonomy can be defined as professional independence and the ability one has to make decisions. Given factors associated with accountability movements, regulations, and policies that impact organizations, autonomy has risen to the top of discussions as a way to ensure that all organization members and leaders are effective, responsive, and treated as highly qualified professionals. Specific to education, Worth and Van den Brande (2020) argue that "Retaining more teachers is crucial for the education system when there are not enough teachers coming into the profession to meet the growing need from rising pupil numbers. Unmanageable workload and low job satisfaction are significant factors determining teachers' decisions to stay in the profession or leave" (p. 3). Worth and Van den Brande (2020) further provide:

Teachers' autonomy over their professional development goal-setting is particularly low, and is the most associated with higher job satisfaction. Increasing teachers' autonomy, particularly over their professional development goals, therefore has great potential for improving teacher job satisfaction and retention. School leaders and the Department for Education should consider how to adapt policy and practice to harness the benefits of teachers having greater involvement in their professional development, goal setting and making decisions. (pp. 3–5)

But autonomy is not only relevant to decisions about professional development and goal setting. Autonomy also pertains to decisions about how to carry out one's job, how to manage the needs of those being served, what resources are needed, and a host of other decisions an organization's members must make in a given day.

Undoubtedly, autonomy impacts job satisfaction, retention, and effectiveness. All professionals want to have input and some control of their professional lives. Given the number of decisions a leader must make, the complex nature of organizations, and the nature of being responsible for leading others, autonomy serves to counterbalance those forces and mitigate them, to an extent, by returning some control to other organization members.

Worth and Van den Brande (2020) conclude that leaders should focus on autonomy and find ways in which organization members can be meaningfully involved and engaged in the way the organization defines its priorities. Autonomy and opportunities for collaborative leadership are fundamental to satisfaction and improvement in outcomes for all organizations.

Resources

Leaders are charged with using resources wisely because for many organizations (and certainly public and educational organizations), resources are finite and often scarce. Leaders cannot create more time in a day; however, they can put measures in place to better use time and to help others do the same. For most leaders, space and financial resources are also finite.

Leadership responsibilities associated with stewardship of resources include resource allocation, resource distribution, the attainment of resources, and the measurement of resource use. Finnigan (2010) asserts that if leaders are to bring about improvement, they must motivate community members by "communicating goals, aligning resources with goals, and fixing problems" (p. 162). This focus on aligning resources with organizational goals relies on strategic and purposeful leadership and stewardship.

Wiseman (2017) posits that many organizations do not have the ability to add resources to tackle real challenges but rather must realign resources and suggests that "the biggest leadership challenge of our times is not insufficient resources per se, but rather our inability to access the most valuable resources" (p. xii). Hoy and Miskel (2013) believe that resources are found to be on a continuum of plentifulness to scarcity and assert that such a continuum is "the extent or capacity of the environment to provide resources that support sustained growth of the organization" (p. 270). People-empowered leaders provide and protect necessary resources so that members of the community can engage in the work of fulfilling the vision and mission of the organization and meeting the needs of those the organization serves.

Stakeholders expect leaders to leverage resources in wise ways. Suskie (2015) argues there is an expectation that leaders act as "wise stewards of their resources, managing and using their resources carefully, responsibly, and judiciously" (p. 59). Leaders must ensure that people in the organization are allocated time and materials to not only get the task done, but to do so in ways that build trust and affirm the value of those the leader serves. Suskie (2015) advocates that leaders should scale back time spent on tangential activities or processes, streamline things that are no longer fully viable, and review time spent on activities that no longer make sense. Suskie (2015) also suggests that leaders should monitor where money is spent, monitor the impact of investment of resources, and deploy resources efficiently.

The strategic allocation and management of resources (e.g., time, space, materials, and budget) has profound impacts on organizations and their outcomes. People-empowered leaders allow others to be part of the discussion on resource allocation and resource attainment. Katzell and Thompson (1990, as cited in Finnigan, 2010) contend that resource adequacy affects motivation and that when resources are not adequately utilized or provided, organization members' motivation is negatively impacted (p. 166). Finnigan (2010) argues that the allocation of resources, in addition to organizational context, leadership, and culture, impacts goals and organizational success (p. 161).

APPLICATIONS TO PROBLEMS OF PRACTICE FOR 21ST-CENTURY LEADERS

Leadership is hard. Leading organizations centered on people brings with it the requirement for leaders to recognize and work through complex needs of people, decisions, relationships, situations, and systems. In addition to complexities, leaders must understand authority, power, and the nuances associated with leading others, building community, maintaining trust, being accountable, and achieving organizational goals. To do this, people-empowered leaders are resolved to serve others, they are committed to leading for the betterment of the organization and not personal glory, and they are focused on people and the strengths and gifts each member of the organization brings to the table.

Understanding Organizational Complexities

Many factors contribute to people-centered systems (such as education and health care organizations) being complex organizations. Mandatory reforms, internal and external politics, accountability models, governance levels and structures (e.g., federal, state, and local), diversity of organizational members, use of resources to meet the needs of all, and accountability to constantly improve create the complex nature of organizations. Kaplan and Owings (2015) provide a model describing the relationship of inputs and outcomes associated with such systems. These open systems are complex and have many different inputs that require leaders to "take inputs from their environment, transform them, and generate outcomes" and describe the inputs as technical capital, human capital, and social capital (p. 93).

Technical capital is one of the inputs that contributes to the complexity associated with people-centered organizations. Given competition over resources, stewardship of resources, and the need for such organizations to meet so many divergent needs, while improving outcomes, leaders are required to make many decisions associated with resource allocation and procurement.

Human capital is also an input that contributes to the complexity of transforming organizations. Leaders and those they serve all come to their role with different capacities, perspectives, and degrees of knowledge. The leader's responsibility is to find congruence and build on those differences to create a richer, more inclusive environment. When someone comes to the organization with high degrees of capacity and knowledge, leaders must value their role in building further capacity among other members. But this use of internal, nonpositional authority can also create challenges that leaders must address.

Social capital inputs of mutual trust, relationships, and shared visions are impactful to organizational outcomes. These types of inputs help form culture. Kaplan and Owings (2015) describe culture as "the way we do things around here" and assert that culture operates "beneath concise awareness" (p. 94).

Table 3.1 Different Types of Capital

Technical Capital	Human Capital	Social Capital
Money and resources needed for transformation or improvement	Knowledge, skills, perspectives, and capacity	Relationships, social networks, trust, and shared commitment to organizational goals

They contend three important assumptions shape culture. These include ideas about those the organization serves, the purpose of the organization, and relationships (p. 97). Because not every member will come to the organization with the same ideas, focus, trust, or desire/skill to build relationships, leaders must acknowledge and help members work through these complex dynamics if an organization's vision is to be realized.

A complex dimension impacting many organizations is the hiring, developing, and retaining of organizational members. Specific to schools is the ability to hire and retain high-quality leaders and teachers that are able to achieve outcomes for all students. Teacher turnover and the rate at which teachers leave the profession all together are among the leading problems facing school leaders and educational systems. The shortage of those needed to support the success of schools and safety of students extends beyond teachers. Schools are experiencing shortages in support staff, building leaders, and even superintendents. These same issues extend to other sectors such as businesses and health care.

A leader's support and a culture that encourages autonomy are central to keeping impactful organization members. Schools provide a clear illustration of this issue. As more and more teachers enter the profession on emergency certifications or through alternative pathways, leaders must embrace training, competency building, and ways to develop teachers while they are learning the profession. Bier (2021) reminds us that "23% of principals and 16% of teachers do not return to their placements from one school year to the next at a cost of nearly $3 billion per year" (p. 27). Education leaders must build those they currently have and create a culture that supports members of the school community.

Effective leaders are able to manage their organizations (complete tasks, refine processes, etc.) and maintain a focus on people. This is not an easy task. However, impactful leaders value those that serve alongside them and lead in ways that support employees, organizational growth, and transformation. A leader's focus on creating a climate of trust, respect, accountability, and mutual commitment toward goals serves as a way to recruit, retain, and grow organizational members.

Understanding Power and Authority

Peopled Leadership seeks to resolve historical thoughts about leadership and the intersection between leadership, people, power, and authority. Authority and power seem similar on the surface, but they are in fact drastically different. Power can be shared, distributed, and allowed to flow between people. Authority cannot. Authority rests with the person who is "in charge," accepts ultimate responsibility, and has been given the position to make decisions and enact policies, processes, and procedures that govern the organization.

Weber (1947/2012) defines power as "the probability that one actor within a social relationship will be in a position to carry out his or her own will despite resistance" (p. 152). Hoy and Miskel (2013) define power as "the ability to get others to do what you want them to do" (p. 231). They also provide:

> Organizations are created and controlled by legitimate authorities, who set goals, design structures, hire and manage employees, and monitor activities to ensure behavior is consistent with the goals and objectives of the organization. These official authorities control the legitimate power of the office or the position, but they are only one of many contenders for other forms of power in the organization. (p. 231)

Hoy and Miskel define authority as the "basis for legitimate control" and that the "primary source of control is formal authority vested in the office or position" (p. 232). They further indicate:

> Authority implies legitimacy, not all power is legitimate. Individuals, groups, or organizations can use power. For example, a department or group can have power, which suggests that it has the ability to influence behavior of other individuals or groups. . . . Likewise, an individual can have power, which indicates success in getting others to comply. (p. 235)

Table 3.2 provides a comparison between power and authority.

French and Snyder (1959) provide a definition of leadership in terms of power and how power is exercised. They suggest:

> Leadership is the potential social influence of one part of the group over another. If one member has power over another, then he has a degree of leadership. Usually, every member has some degree of influence over others in an

Table 3.2 Power and Authority

	Power	Authority
Definition	The capacity a person or group has to influence another person or group.	A formal position of influence and responsibility.
Legitimacy	No	Yes
Derived from	Personal influence, expertise, innovation, charisma, personal relationships.	Title, appointment, specific position or office.
Hierarchy status	Flows in any direction and is not hierarchical.	Specific to a person and/or position and is hierarchical.

informal group; in other words, the leadership is distributed throughout the group. (p. 118)

Peopled leaders acknowledge that everyone in the organization can have social influence over other members. They further recognize the power and leadership abilities of others and harness both to move the organization forward. These leaders seek to distribute power, leadership experiences, and opportunities to organization members in order to share in leadership. French and Raven (1959) provide a theory of power and its relationship to leadership. Their theory helps leaders gain an understanding of the nature of differing types of power as a mechanism by which to lead organization members. French and Raven assert that "The processes of power are pervasive, complex, and often distinguished in our society" (p. 150) and identify that the main purpose for studying types of power is to "define them systematically so that we may compare them according to the changes they will produce and other effects which accompany the use of power" (p. 150).

French and Raven (1959) also argue that "The phenomena of power and influence involves a dyadic relation between two agents, which may be viewed from two points of view: (a) What determines the behavior of the agent who exerts power? (b) What determines the reactions of the recipient of the behavior?" (p. 150). The ability to understand power from each perspective is foundational to relationships in open social systems, building and maintaining trust, empowering others, and allowing members of the organization to act autonomously, in support of agreed-upon goals. Peopled leaders understand how, to what extent, and when to lead from differing bases of power.

The five bases of power outlined by French and Raven (1959) include reward power, coercive power, legitimate power, referent power, and expert power (pp. 155–156). Reward power is described as power that stems from the ability to give a reward. French and Raven suggest:

> The use of rewards to change systems within the range of reward power tends to increase reward power by increasing the probability attached to future promise. However, unsuccessful attempts to exert reward power outside the range of power would tend to decrease the power. (pp. 156–157)

French and Raven believe that reward power and coercive power share similarities in that the basis of the power is in "the ability to manipulate the attainment of valences" (p. 157). In the case of reward power, the power hinges on rewards or perceived rewards, and with coercive power, punishment or the threat of punishment is the basis of power.

French and Raven (1959) additionally provide a definition of legitimate power and contend that such power stems from three bases: cultural values, acceptance of social structure, and a designation as a legitimizing authority (p. 160). They argue that legitimate power stems from internalized values of the person being influenced by the power agent, regard for the influence of the power agent, and the obligation the person feels to accept influence. Referent power is based on a "feeling of oneness" between people, a "desire to become closely associated," and a "feeling of membership or a desire to join" (p. 161). French and Raven note that expert power is dependent on others' perception that the power agent has expertise, cognitive knowledge, and superior ability (p. 164). They also provide that when one attempts to exert expert power outside of actual ability of expert knowledge, an "undermining of confidence" occurs.

Weber (1947/2012) distinguishes between three differing types of authority: charismatic authority, traditional authority, and legal authority. Hoy and Miskel (2013) describe charismatic authority as authority that "rests on devotion to an extraordinary individual who is leader by virtue of person, trust, or exemplary qualities" (p. 231). Traditional authority is defined by Hoy and Miskel as being "anchored in an established belief in sanctity of the status of those exercising authority" (p. 231) and that obedience is grounded in the position and the person who occupies the position. Legal authority is described by Hoy and Miskel as "authority based on enacted laws" and that "obedience is not owed to a person or position but to the laws that specify to whom and to what extent people owe compliance" (p. 232).

Peabody (1962) conducted a study focusing on organizational authority and outlined two types of authority, formal and functional. Peabody concluded that "authority is initially based on formal position, legitimacy, and the sanctions inherent in office, its acceptance is conditioned by several additional factors" (p. 465), which he notes are professional competence, experience, and leadership. Hoy and Miskel (2013) describe formal authority as being based on "legitimacy and position," while functional authority is described as being based on "competence and personal human relation skills" (p. 232). Peopled leaders take these types of authorities into account and find balance with what the organization and its members need.

Kovach (2020) notes that different types of power can be used in different situations and asserts that the way a leader uses different types of power is key in relationships between the leader and organization members. Kovach argues:

> The behavior of a supervisor is reflected by a number of circumstances including: 1) the current professional relationship with his or her individual employees and team collectively, 2) the attitude and loyalty the employees have towards

this supervisor (or organization), 3) the ability to be (and feel) successful, 4) previous outcomes based on similar experiences within the organization, and 5) the supervisor's motivation to be successful. (pp. 2–3)

The premise argued is that leaders must respond with knowledge of and care for their organization members and an understanding that their leadership and relationships matter to the success of the organization and its members. Kovach further contends that

[Leaders] who positively influence employees are likely to produce positive outcomes. The same idea is true for leaders who negatively use influence on employees—they are likely to produce negative outcomes. These outcomes result from the power exhibited upon the employee. Thus, employee motivation can be altered based on the type of power his or her supervisor exhibits. (p. 8)

Knowing this, people-empowered leaders take the opportunity to celebrate success, reward employees, and appreciate members of the organization with true gratitude.

A people-empowered leader achieves organizational goals and fulfills the organization's vision and mission through awareness of how to use authority, how to empower people with leadership opportunities, and when and how to distribute power. While never relinquishing their authority, impactful leaders do share power. That power is multiplied the more they share it. We no longer live in a world where leadership is solely dependent on one's position. We are now in a world where we know that it takes all the people of an organization to achieve a set vision, make gains, and create success. Positional leaders, the ones with authority, are ultimately responsible for the success or failure of the organization and readily accept that responsibility. However, they attribute the success of the organization to the people and give them credit for achieving the vision and mission of the organization.

BRIDGING THE GAP BETWEEN RESEARCH AND PRACTICE

At the center of this phase of the *Peopled Leadership* model, people empowered, lies leader humility. Empowering organization members, providing a culture of autonomy, and ensuring members have resources are foundational aspects to being a people-empowered leader. Admitting mistakes, asking for help, allowing others to lead, knowing the leader cannot do it alone, leaning on others, and acting with the heart of a leader who allows members to shine and take credit for success is the very essence of a people-empowered leader.

The complexities associated with people-centered organizations are abundant. People-empowered leaders know this and work to mitigate the chaos often associated with open systems. They accept the nuances and have an "all-hands-on-deck" approach to mitigating the complexities and staying focused on the vision, mission, and goals at the heart of the organization. A leader's knowledge of how to use authority to help the organization achieve desired outcomes, an understanding of the exercise of power and influence, and creating a culture of shared power and influence are fundamental to leading people in ways that respect their expertise, experience, and commitment. People-empowered leaders know that people are the heart of an organization, and they empower them to achieve greatness.

CASE STUDY

You have interviewed for a leadership position in a specific section, within a state department. You are excited about the prospect of this leadership position because it has meaningful outreach and the opportunity to impact an entire state and those the department serves. This position will also provide you with the opportunity to manage a rather large budget, lead a team of 34 employees (varying from three weeks to 40 years in the department), lead new state initiatives, engage with other departments, create new processes, and work with leaders across the state to bring about change and "move the needle forward."

During the final interview, the committee was very honest about some of the challenges associated with this position, some of which include:

- inadequate departmental budget;
- outdated and ineffective processes;
- low employee morale;
- instances of poor customer service;
- inadequate internal and external communication that negatively impacts the department;
- a lack of trust by some stakeholders and influential groups;
- high-stakes accountability and reporting to the legislature, governor, oversight boards, accreditors, and the federal government;
- new initiatives, some of which are controversial; and
- the bureaucracy associated with state work in general.

You were also informed about some of the strengths of your team, which include:

- deep institutional knowledge,
- an excitement about new leadership,
- comradery among team members,
- a recognition for the need for change, and
- a willingness for team members to share opinions and ideas.

You are undaunted and believe you are up to the challenge. Once you left the interview, you began to really think about how you would handle some of those challenges and draw on some of the strengths.

Several weeks later, you received notice that you are the chosen candidate for the position; you happily decided to accept the offer. The executive director (who is the person to whom you report) had you come in to meet and gave you a file of information believed to be important as you begin this new role. Some of the information included is a department policy manual, organizational chart, copy of the budget, employment and performance records, results of the last department survey of both employees and stakeholders, copies of the most pressing polices that impact your team, the strategic plan for the section, and outline of some of the new initiatives for which you and your team will be responsible. Responding to the information you were given and the challenges you were informed about during the interview process, you were asked to draft a 30- and 90-day plan that will guide your work over the first three months.

Two more weeks passed, and you began this exciting new position. On your first day, you spent some time getting to know your new team, engaging with other directors, and meeting with your executive director to discuss your plan of action.

DISCUSSION QUESTIONS

1. Which of the challenges will you prioritize? Why?
2. Are there other additional pieces of data or information you might request?
3. What is your first 30-day plan? Your first 90-day plan?
4. What are some challenges you might experience with getting people onboard with things that need to change?
5. How will you draw on the strengths of your team?
6. How can you distribute power? What powers are appropriate to distribute?
7. How will you empower the people on your team?
8. How would the practice of humility promote the effectiveness of your leadership?

9. What will you do to ensure your team and department move beyond meeting expectations and ensure you and your team exceed them?

REFERENCES

Bier, M. (2021). Servant leadership for schools. *Journal of Character Education, 17*(2), 27–46.

Chiu, T., & Hung, Y. (2020). Impacts of leader humility between authority and trustworthiness on compliance: Test of three-way interactions. *Psychological Reports, 125*(1), 398–421.

Dubrin, A. (2007). *Leadership research findings, practice, and skills.* Houghton Mifflin.

Finnigan, K. (2010). Principal leadership and teacher motivation under high stakes accountability policies. *Leadership and Policy in Schools, 9*, 161–189.

French, J., and Raven, B. (1959). The bases of social power. In D. Cartwright (Ed.), *Studies in social power* (pp. 150–165). Research Center for Group Dynamics Institute for Social Research, University of Michigan.

French, J., and Snyder, R. (1959). Leadership and interpersonal power. In D. Cartwright (Ed.), *Studies in social power* (pp. 118–149). Research Center for Group Dynamics Institute for Social Research, University of Michigan.

Frostenson, M. (2016). Humility in business: A contextual approach. *Journal of Business Ethics, 138*, 91–102.

Hoy, W. K., & Miskel, C. G. (2013). *Educational administration: Theory, research, and practice* (9th ed.). McGraw-Hill.

Kaplan, L. S., & Owings, W. A. (2015). *Introduction to the principalship: Theory to practice.* Routledge.

Kouzes, J., & Posner, B. (2012). *The leadership challenge: How to make extraordinary things happen in organizations* (5th ed.). Jossey-Bass.

Kovach, M. (2020). Leader influence: A research review of French and Raven's (1959) power dynamics. *The Journal of Values-Based Leadership, 13*(2). https://doi.org/10.22543/0733.132.1312

Leithwood, K., & Mascall, B. (2008). Collective leadership effects on student achievement. *Educational Administration Quarterly, 44*(4), 529–561.

Owens, B., Johnson, M., & Mitchell, T. (2013). Expressed humility in organizations: Implications for performance, teams and leadership. *Organizational Science, 24*(5), 1517–1538.

Peabody, R. (1962). Perceptions of organizational authority: A comparative analysis. *Administrative Science Quarterly, 6*, 463–482.

Sebastian, J., Allensworth, E., & Huang, H. (2016, November). The role of teacher leadership in how principals influence classroom instruction and student learning. *American Journal of Education, 123*(1), 69–108. https://www.journals.uchicago.edu/doi/epdf/10.1086/688169

Suda, L. (2013). In praise of followers. Paper presented at PMI® Global Congress 2013—North America, New Orleans, LA. Newtown Square, PA: Project

Management Institute. https://www.pmi.org/learning/library/importance-of -effective-followers-5887

Suskie, L. (2015). *Five dimensions of quality: A common sense guide to accreditation and accountability.* Jossey-Bass.

Urban, E. (2019, August 9). Five ways leaders can embrace empowerment to build high-performing teams. *Forbes.* https://www.forbes.com/sites/ forbescoachescouncil/2019/08/09/five-ways-leaders-can-embrace-empowerment -to-build-high-performing-teams/?sh=6a2459993b0c

Weber, M. (2012). *The theory of social and economic organization* (A. M. Henderson, Ed., & T. Parsons, Trans.). Martino Fine Books. (Original work published 1947)

Wiseman, L. (2017). *Multipliers: How the very best leaders make everyone smarter.* HarperCollins.

Worth, J., and Van den Brande, J. (2020). *Teacher autonomy: How does it relate to job satisfaction and retention?* National Foundation for Education Research. https: //files.eric.ed.gov/fulltext/ED604418.pdf

Chapter 4

Peopled Leadership

People Transformed

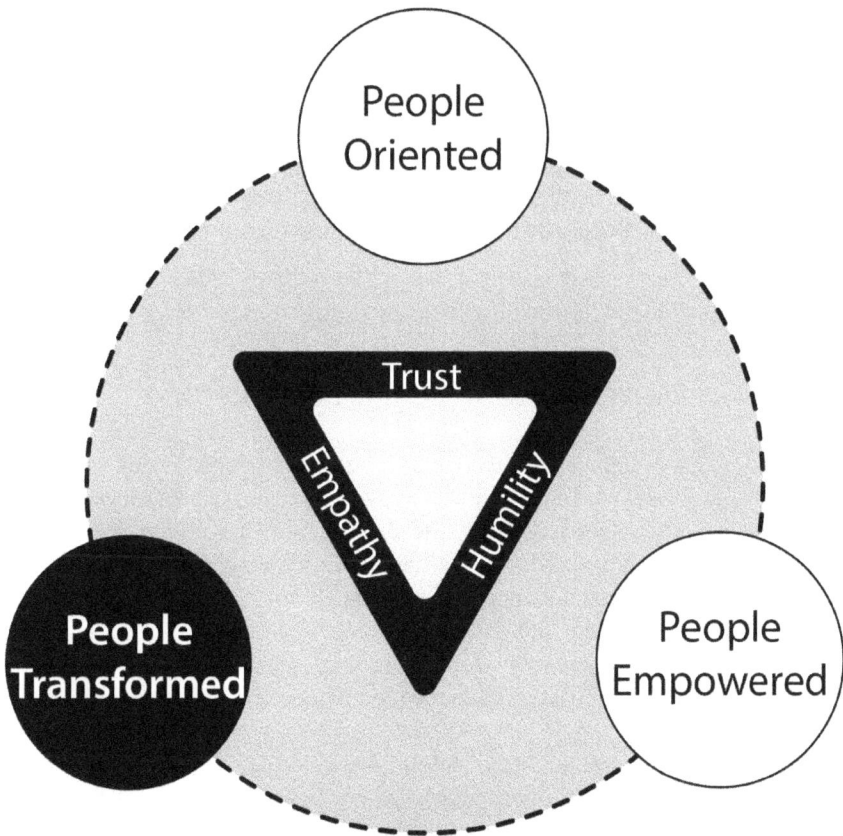

Fig. 4.1. *Peopled Leadership*: People Transformed. *Jack Ousey.*

Those who want to lead a dynamic organization that is typified by quality of service and top-notch results realize that good relationships are critical not only to their personal success but to the success of the organization as well. However, looming large in the leader's mind is the constant concern about results. In a school setting, these concerns include test scores, student safety, retention of key employees, and support for teachers. In a business setting, leaders focus on profitability, company growth, and remaining relevant in the marketplace. For those who lead faith-based organizations, important issues include congregational growth, leading in a spiritually effective way, and care for the attendees.

At times, it is with trepidation that leaders are faced with a nagging question about how to spend or focus the majority of their time in order to be effective, thereby leading the organization to quality results. The peopled leader remains focused on people. Once trust is established and the leader is in a position to allow others to emerge as leaders themselves, the last phase of *Peopled Leadership* is People Transformed, sustaining an organization of transformed individuals, thus transforming the organization. Building and maintaining strong interpersonal relationships among employees is the firm foundation upon which transformed people thrive and produce transformed organizations. Ziglar (2000) observed: "I believe that you can get everything in life you want if you will just help enough other people get what they want" (p. 117). The theoretical bases for the third phase of the *Peopled Leadership* model, People Transformed, are emotional intelligence and servant leadership.

BASIC PRINCIPLES OF
PEOPLE-TRANSFORMED LEADERSHIP

The third phase of the *Peopled Leadership* model is People Transformed. In this phase, the leader has transitioned to a role primarily of a behind-the-scenes facilitator because other leaders in the organization have emerged. In this phase, the organization begins to exhibit three major characteristics. First, organization members take increased responsibility for planning, problem solving, decision-making, and carrying out other needed tasks. Organization members often form their own working groups, seek out their own needed professional development and other needed resources, including help from each other.

The second characteristic of people-transformed leadership is the leader becomes less differentiated particularly within but also outside of the organization. This means levels of trust in the organization are so deep that all members have the confidence to participate in frank discussions about issues or problems the organization faces. In other words, organization members are confident in the security and safety of the organizational environment to take risks and make themselves vulnerable. By facilitating the creation of this kind of environment, the leader has flattened the hierarchy, elevating organization members in the process. Although there are still a few decisions the leader cannot delegate, the leader has become more difficult to readily identify, particularly from outside of the organization.

The third major characteristic of the People Transformed phase of leadership is the organization's ability to quickly and decisively address the unexpected challenges so frequently encountered in the 21st-century workplace. In 2020, a worldwide pandemic turned lives and workplaces upside down. A new lexicon of social distancing, facemask wearing, and curbside pickup at businesses appeared overnight. The concept of the workplace was turned on its head. Later in this chapter, we will examine how an organization transformed through *Peopled Leadership* is uniquely positioned to respond to such challenges.

DISCUSSION OF RELEVANT RESEARCH

Too many leaders find themselves in a quandary when establishing their priorities. In his book *Trust and Inspire*, Covey (2022) describes the dilemma in this way:

> Leaders need to perform to get results. . . . Leaders know they are responsible for their own performance as well as for the results their team produces. And they are responsible for the *outcomes*, not just the activities. The very best leaders know they need *both* to get results *and* to build the relationship. Unwittingly, too many leaders get trapped in the following false dichotomy: *Do I complete the task . . . or build the relationship?* (p. 181)

Peopled leaders understand the answer is both. Developing high levels of emotional intelligence provides the avenue through which these tasks are successfully completed.

Emotional Intelligence

Doing the hard work of maintaining relationships necessary to sustain the synergy of a transformed organization requires the leader to be attuned to the emotional needs of organization members. Mayer and Salovey (1997) defined emotional intelligence as:

> The ability to perceive accurately, appraise, and express emotion; the ability to access and/or generate feelings when they facilitate thought; the ability to understand emotion and emotional knowledge; and the ability to regulate emotions to promote emotional and intellectual growth. (p. 10)

According to Goleman (1998), emotional intelligence "refers to the capacity for recognizing our own feelings and those of others, for motivating ourselves, and for managing emotions well in ourselves and in our relationships" (p. 317). In his emotional competence framework, Goleman (1998) identified the personal competence of self-awareness and the social competence of empathy as key components of emotional intelligence. Goleman also estimated that "close to 90% of a leader's success is attributable to emotional intelligence" (p. 34).

Nelson and Low (2011) believe that emotional intelligence helps leaders to identify, comprehend, and value the needs and goals of those they lead and that "emotional intelligence is the single most important variable influencing personal achievement, career success, leadership, and life satisfaction (p. xxiii). These successes on the individual level can translate to success on the organizational level. Connors (2021) explains the link between emotional intelligence and high-performing leaders:

> Emotional intelligence, or EQ, is the predictor that distinguishes outstanding performers and leaders from the average. More than any other skill, EQ helps you build *transformative* relationships throughout your organization, whatever your role may be. A deeper understanding of yourself heightens your awareness of your own needs, as well as the needs of those you lead. Understanding how and why your emotions influence your behavior helps you make more intelligent decisions, enabling you to identify opportunities that become game changers for your business. (p. xi)

Emotional intelligence may be the best predictor of long-term success for leaders in the workplace. Connors (2021) believes that "wise, practical leaders understand how to use emotional intelligence to grow their business, boost their career prospects, and create future successful leaders" (p. xi).

Emotional intelligence is particularly important in the context of current leadership challenges. Goodlet et al. (2022) identified resilience and emotional intelligence as key tools to maintaining positive mental health and managing anxiety, particularly during times of great stress, such as in the midst of a pandemic. They concluded that emotional intelligence is linked to "decreased burnout, greater organizational commitment, and proactive implementation of positive coping strategies in response to stressful situations" (p. 32).

Salovey and Mayer (1990) proposed a comprehensive theory of emotional intelligence that focuses on the use of feelings to guide thought and action. In this model, Salovey and Mayer define emotional intelligence in terms of being able to monitor and regulate one's own feelings as well as being sensitive to the feelings of others. They also theorized that the management of one's own emotions develops over time as a person matures.

Although the idea of emotional intelligence has its roots in the work of Thorndike in the 1920s (Kearney et al., 2014), a robust body of research has been produced recently. This research examines the relationship of emotional intelligence to various leadership models (Dåderman et al., 2013; Harms & Credé, 2010; Yukl & Mahsud, 2010), benefits of emotional intelligence for leaders (Abdullahi et al., 2020; Fix & Atnafou-Boyer, 2022; Gómez-Leal et al., 2022; Kaur & Hirudayaraj, 2021; Labby et al., 2013; Parrish, 2015), and emotional intelligence as applied to current challenges of leadership (Chaudhary et al., 2022; Goodlet et al., 2022; Wirawan et al., 2018; Wittmer & Hopkins, 2021).

Relationship of Emotional Intelligence to Leadership

Recent research suggests emotional intelligence is related to transformational leadership. Gómez-Leal et al. (2022) found correlations between emotional intelligence and the constructs of transformational leadership. Using a leadership intelligence questionnaire, Dåderman et al. (2013) concluded that emotional intelligence, social intelligence, and spiritual intelligence were related to transformational leadership. They found that emotional intelligence supported relationship building, rational intelligence assisted with problem solving, and spiritual intelligence provided the basis for creating a vision that includes ethical values.

Harms and Credé (2010) also found a relationship between emotional intelligence and transformational leadership, particularly in the areas of encouraging learning, acting as role models, and building trust. Yukl and Mahsud (2010) concluded that emotional intelligence was related to flexible and adaptive leadership because of the role of emotional intelligence in facilitating change both internal and external to the organization.

Benefits of Emotional Intelligence for Leaders

Research has provided evidence that emotional intelligence provides many benefits for leaders and those whom they lead. Kaur and Hirudayaraj (2021) view emotional intelligence as "the ability to use a rational mind and emotions simultaneously" (p. 52). This ability allows leaders to create and maintain a psychologically safe work environment, support decision-making, and facilitate collaboration. Labby et al. (2013) found emotional intelligence helps leaders improve as listeners and communicators, which in turn, means the leaders are better equipped to support positive mental health of those they lead through the creating and maintaining of a healthy work climate.

Parrish (2015) examined the relevance of emotional intelligence in academic leadership: "the study identified emotional intelligence traits related to empathy, inspiring and guiding others, and responsibly managing oneself and most applicable for academic leadership" (p. 829). Within the construct of empathy, Parrish found that leaders with strong emotional intelligence tended to exhibit greater integrity than other leaders. The benefits also allow leaders to "ensure that each member of their team has the necessary resources, skills, and capacity to accomplish the negotiated goals" (p. 831). Gómez-Leal et al.'s (2022) work provides further support for the conclusion that leaders with strong emotional intelligence tend to also be leaders of integrity and transparency.

Emotional Intelligence and Emerging Leadership Challenges

Recent research has examined the benefits of emotional intelligence for leadership by addressing emerging challenges such as pandemics and the increase in remote work by employees. Goodlet et al. (2022) examined the impact of the COVID-19 pandemic on the emotional intelligence of students enrolled in a pharmacy program. Results indicate increased levels of emotional intelligence among the students led to the maintenance of positive relationships in the program. This result was attributed to students "taking the time to understand where others are coming from, extending grace and empathy toward others instead of rushing to judgment, and making an active effort to maintain personal relationships and show people you care" (p. 34). Social awareness and listening skills were also found to have been improved.

One of the results of the recent pandemic was the emergence of remote working. Currently, 58.6% of the American workforce works remotely at least in some part while 41% work fully remotely. Prior to the pandemic, only 7% of the American workforce worked from home (Anderson, n.d.). Leadership of remote workers is still an emerging area of research. Wittmer and Hopkins (2021) examined the effects of emotional intelligence and leading those who work remotely. Specifically, the areas of self-perception, self-expression, interpersonal relationships, decision-making, and stress management were reviewed. All of these areas of emotional intelligence were found to be critical to those who lead remote workers. These areas provide the basis for maintaining trust and healthy work relationships.

Chaudhary et al. (2022) researched the impact of leader's e-competencies on employees' well-being in global virtual teams during a pandemic. Results indicate emotional intelligence helps increase leaders' ability in three core areas: e-communication skills, e-change management skills, and e-technical skills. These increased skills led to increased levels of well-being among remote employees. Chaudhary et al. (2022) concluded:

> The degree of the positive impact of leaders' e-competencies will be high on employees' wellbeing in the presence of emotional intelligence in e-leaders. Furthermore, leaders who exhibit appropriate emotional management have proven to be more effective in handling employee wellbeing concerns. (p. 1057)

Emotional intelligence provides many tools for the peopled leader. These tools include the ability to monitor the emotional well-being and health of the relationships within the team. Peopled leaders place the needs of team members at the center of their "radar screens" and work to ensure their needs are fulfilled. Relationship-centered, people-transformed leadership is thus closely related to servant leadership (Wirawan et al., 2018), the other half of the theoretical basis for phase three of *Peopled Leadership*.

Servant Leadership

Related to transformational leadership and emotional intelligence, servant leadership is based on the belief that true leaders put others' needs at the top of their priorities so that team members are empowered to be leaders in their own areas. Although the idea of servant leadership has been around for many years, Greenleaf (1977) was among the first to formally promote servant leadership as a generally viable model of leadership: "The servant-leader is servant first. . . . It begins with the natural feeling that one wants to serve, to serve *first*" (p. 27, emphasis in the original). Greenleaf also indicates what sets servant leadership apart is "the care taken by the servant-leader to make sure that other people's highest priority needs are being served" and the best test is to ask, "Do those being served grow as persons?" (p. 27).

Research concerning servant leadership has identified important benefits for leaders of all kinds of organizations. Kim et al. (2021) concluded that servant leadership has a positive impact on team members' perceptions of the support provided them by the organization, on team members' belief in their own empowerment and on the team's ability to manage change. Wallace et al. (2022) concluded that servant leaders understand individual differences, possess integrity, build trust, and understand and value relationships. Further, they concluded that commitment to the principles of servant leadership and to the organization and its members was the essential element to the underpinning of successful leadership.

Kiker et al. (2019) concluded that servant leadership is strongly associated with task-related job performance and organizational citizenship behavior.

Ghalavi and Nastiezaie (2020) found a strong, positive correlation between servant leadership and organizational citizenship behavior, suggesting servant leadership is an effective way to create a climate that supports productive behaviors of team members. They also found a positive and significant relationship between servant leadership and empowerment, suggesting servant leadership is also an effective tool for building empowerment in team members.

Bramlett (2018) has articulated 12 competencies of servant leaders. Of the 12, four stand out as essential elements of building relationships: listening, empathy, acting with humility, and building a culture of trust. Leaders who focus their efforts on these and other concepts related to the *Peopled Leadership* presented in this book will see an ordinary organization transformed into an extraordinary team that is characterized by sincerity, honesty, and compassion, which translates into organizational effectiveness and quality results.

APPLICATIONS TO PROBLEMS OF PRACTICE

Leading any organization in this current era of change might cause some to reconsider their career choice and run back to the safe confines of their previous position. Being promoted to a position of greater responsibility ultimately leads to higher pay, but once there, some inevitably ask themselves, "Now what?" In today's climate of turmoil and unrest, otherwise common challenges tend to become extraordinary in scope. The challenges addressed in this section are managing change, finding time to listen, and facilitating problem solving.

Managing Change

Years ago, in *Managing at the Speed of Change*, Conner (1992) wrote, "Never before has so much changed so fast and with such dramatic implications for the entire world" (p. 3). This challenge was echoed by Kriegel and Brandt (1996): "Future changes will be bigger and come faster because the rate of change grows exponentially, not incrementally" (p. 3). The last 25 years of history have borne out Kriegel and Brandt's prediction. In 1900, human knowledge doubled about every 100 years. By 1945, the doubling rate of knowledge was down to 45 years. As of 2021, best estimates suggest knowledge is doubling every 12 hours (Lodestar Solutions, n.d.). In 2012, one exabyte (about 1 billion gigabytes) of data was generated each day. Data specialists are predicting that within the next five years, we will be measuring data in yottabytes (one million exabytes), the largest unit yet approved by the

International System of Units (Gillis, 2022). When coupled with the inability to ensure the accuracy, not to mention the trustworthiness, of so much information available, managing change is an increasingly daunting challenge.

A consultant who helps develop emerging leaders through an online coaching initiative called LEAP, or Leadership Acceleration Program, Silsbee (2015) identified seven challenges embedded in managing change that appeared over and over when it comes to coaching leaders for organizational success:

1. Isolation.
2. Lack of honest feedback.
3. Lack of emotional intelligence.
4. Leading from a place of influence rather than authority.
5. Leading and managing change effectively.
6. Communication.
7. Thinking about the big picture and systematically. (para. 1)

The stress and turmoil that the pandemic of 2020 brought to leaders of a variety of different organizations representing many areas of concern have been discussed elsewhere in this book. This rapid change of pace and severity of impact has caused chaos on a wide and unprecedented level. Considering all the changes and upheavals society has experienced in just the past 10 years, it is easy to understand what Benjamin Franklin meant when he offered the following observation: "Change is the only constant in life. One's ability to adapt to those changes will determine your success in life."

Because of the deep levels of trust built in the People Oriented phase and nurtured through the People Empowered phase, organizations of transformed team members are ideally positioned to "pivot on a dime" when conditions require such quick movement. Team members can not only be depended on to have the skills and preparation to do their part, but they can also be depended on to provide support for others that need it. Often, this means stepping out of one's comfort zone to quickly acquire a new skill or take on a new task. Because of deep-seated trust in the organization, leaders can ask these things of team members, and neither the need nor the wisdom tends to be questioned.

As excellence in leadership is pursued, Maxwell's thoughts are informative: "Competency goes beyond words. It's the leader's ability to say it, plan it, and do it in such a way that others know that you know how—and know that they want to follow you" (Searchquotes, n.d.). People-transformed leaders have moved beyond mere competence. They have created an organization whose members have the skills to say it, plan it, and do it. The leader builds the trust and autonomy to let those skills serve the organization at their own initiative. This kind of organization requires strong relationships built on trust. The keys to building and maintaining the relationships are emotional intelligence and servant leadership.

Finding the Time to Listen

Lack of trust is a major obstacle to building relationships. Oftentimes, people spend their time trying to figure out what the other person is really trying to say in a conversation. Listening with your heart in addition to your ears seems to be a lost art and leads to a lack of empathy. Davidson (1989) so eloquently stated: "People may forget what you said, but they will never forget how you made them feel" (p. 21). When we convey to other colleagues that we truly care about them as people, transformed relationships are the result, and this leads to a deeper commitment to the organization. Employees will look forward to working with others who understand them and truly care about them as individuals.

In a book about achieving success one conversation at a time, Scott (2004) identified seven principles of fierce conversations. Principle #3 advises the learner to "be here, prepared to be nowhere else" when participating in communication that is intentional (p. 91). Included in the debrief that everyone should ask of themselves after participating in a conversation are three critical questions:

1. Was I genuinely curious about this person and his or her reality?
2. Did feelings get expressed, as well as issues and solutions?
3. Who did most of the talking? "Me" is the wrong answer. (Scott, 2004, p. 113)

Clearly, emotional intelligence involves the closely related concepts of sensitivity to and empathy for others. One question that people who have a high EQ (emotional quotient) constantly ask themselves is this: How am I being perceived by the other person in this or any conversation? Clear, accurate communication will occur when these elements are considered and will soon become second nature for anyone who adjusts their personal approach to dealing with others. Mark Twain once said, "It's better to remain silent and let everyone around you think you're a fool as opposed to opening your mouth and removing all doubt."

Listening is a skill that should come easier than it does. Each human customarily has two ears and one mouth, indicating that maybe we should listen twice as much as we speak. Truly great, transformed leaders are those who have developed well-honed listening skills that enable them to hear what other people are saying and help them meet their needs.

At the heart of every good relationship is a sincere desire for genuine fellowship, which is grounded in mutual respect, trust, sensitivity, and empathy for others. Good personal relationships, like anything else that is worthwhile in life, are like cheese: They get better with time. A critical component of relationships is empathy, for when people communicate the idea that they understand how other people feel and can sympathize with what they are experiencing, a very real dialogue begins to emerge. True yet simple communication starts to occur on a regular basis as one person realizes the other person "gets me."

An old Indian proverb recommends: "Let me not cast judgment on my brother until I have walked a mile in his moccasins" (author unknown). It is impossible to comprehend how another person feels unless you yourself have struggled under the weight of a similar problem. Compassion is evident when sympathy prevails. Likewise, people do not care how much you know until they know how much you care.

Peopled leaders are, by definition, good listeners. They listen because they care about their people as individuals. Peopled leaders listen intently with their ears but also with their eyes. Observing facial expressions and body language is an important listening skill. Perhaps even more important is the understanding when the aural data (listening with one's ears) and the visual data (listening with one's eyes) are sending inconsistent messages. By building trust in the People Oriented phase and nurturing that trust in the People Empowered phase, leaders of transformed organizations make finding time to listen a priority and then use the resulting data to address the members' needs based on that data.

People Transformed leadership requires leaders who are empathetic and feel the burdens of their subordinates. They can put themselves in the shoes of their employees and see the world through their eyes. A very real focus comes into view as leaders see their efforts as being instrumental in providing a workplace that is characterized by high levels of trust, which lead to greater autonomy.

History has revealed that great leaders have had an awareness of others and were sensitive to their needs. Many of these are found in the spiritual realm. One of the best examples of this attitude is recorded in the Gospel of Mark where Jesus Christ spoke these immortal words: "Whoever wants to become great among you shall be your servant" (Mark 10:43). Hindu leader Swami Vivekananda wrote, "He who is the servant of all is their true master." In Judaism, "to lead is to serve. Those who serve do not lift themselves high. They lift other people high."

Greenleaf (1991, pp. 9–20) identified the following elements as critical components of servant leadership:

- Listening
- Empathy
- Healing (of self and others)
- Awareness of others, situations, and self
- Persuasion
- Conceptualization
- Foresight
- Stewardship
- Commitment to the growth of others
- Building community

It has often been said that the secret to happiness is hard to figure out, but the secret to unhappiness is easy—just get too focused on yourself. John Rockefeller serves as an example for this perspective. Most students of history can easily identify him as one of the great business success stories of the early 20th century as he led Standard Oil to prominence during a time of great advancement in American society. However, many people are surprised to hear about his near death at the age of 47 as he was acquiring a position of wealth and influence that not even he could have imagined.

With that great wealth and stature came tremendous pressure to perform amid continued guidance for a company that earned enormous profits. Due to the stress of his job, he developed ulcers and began to lose weight. Insomnia set in as he spent many a sleepless night trying to figure out what to do as he anticipated problems that were imaginary and nonexistent. Doctors were consulted, and he was told that he should get his affairs in order, for the time of his death was near. Rockefeller once said about this time in his life that "all the fortune that I have made has not served to compensate me for the anxiety of that period" (Chernow, 1998).

But something strange happened. The desire to live became a strong focus for Rockefeller. He began to wonder if there was something he could do that might prevent his early death. Through much thought and prayer, he decided to give some of his enormous wealth to those in need, and he began to share his resources with the poor. Little by little, his health began to improve and he started sleeping better. The doctors were amazed at his recovery and saw that his desire to help others played a crucial role in the healing process.

John Rockefeller lived to be 97 years young. In his memoirs, he credited this turnaround in his life to a simple thought that he discovered while reading scripture: "Tis more blessed to give than to receive." Of interesting note to this story is the fact that the Rockefeller family has contributed great amounts of money to worthy causes around the world and this change in seeking to serve others probably saved his life.

Buckingham and Coffman (1999) interviewed over 80,000 managers from companies of different sizes in a multiyear survey that was designed to identify what great managers have in common. Their research led to the following 12 questions that are prevalent in the minds of employees:

1. Do I know what is expected of me at work?
2. Do I have the equipment and material I need to do my work right?
3. At work, do I have the opportunity to do what I do best every day?
4. In the last seven days, have I received recognition or praise for good work?
5. *Does my supervisor or someone at work seem to care about me as a person?* (Emphasis added)
6. Is there someone at work who encourages my development?
7. At work, do my opinions seem to count?
8. Does the mission/purpose of my company make me feel my work is important?
9. Are my co-workers committed to doing quality work?
10. *Do I have a best friend at work?* (Emphasis added)
11. In the last six months, have I talked to someone about my progress?
12. This last year, have I had opportunities at work to learn and grow?

Questions 5 and 10 from this list are typical of the concepts related to building good relationships and are indicative of quality personal interactions that are meaningful and purpose driven and lead to emotional well-being. This list is mentioned here for the purpose of illustrating the importance of taking time to care for others. This mindset of putting the needs of others before their very own is what 21st-century leaders do, and it serves to transform the organizations they lead.

Problem Solving

Quality problem-solving skills involve a strong knowledge of the cognitive domain of Bloom's Taxonomy. Bloom (1956) developed a taxonomy that is based on six levels of thinking. The first three levels of Bloom's Taxonomy focus on the foundational components of knowledge, understanding, and application. Knowledge is simply the recall of certain facts and elements related to what was read or heard. Understanding occurs when a learner not only receives knowledge about an idea or concept but also can describe or explain how the information can be used. Application happens when knowledge and understanding are used or "applied" to an event in a way that causes improvement and allows for clarity.

Bloom (1956) explained that each level of this model builds from the level beneath it and a learner cannot develop a better understanding of a concept without first experiencing the foundational elements before progressing to the higher components of the model. Therefore, the concepts of analysis, synthesis, and evaluation are associated with higher-order thinking skills that require individuals to think critically about the information they have received and determine how that information can be best utilized. Analysis allows learners to make connections between ideas, whereas synthesis enables people to take a stand on an issue as they seek to defend their position on a matter. However, at the apex of this learning model sits the concept of evaluation.

Evaluation occurs when learners set about the actions of solving, appraising, justifying, and assessing what is best for *them*. This level is also the point where emotions become involved, for without emotional attachment, there is no deep learning. Evaluation causes action since a person has been so moved by a new, deeper level of comprehension, which leads to activity or taking a firm stand on a matter. This evaluative process involves the emotions and is generally characterized by combining the various elements of knowledge, skills, facts, and logic to make unique personal judgments. Consequently, when a person experiences learning at the highest level of Bloom's Taxonomy, it becomes transformational. It is at this point where the new learning prompts individuals to risk the possibility of rejection as they seek to assess the well-being of a colleague, friend, coworker, or associate. However, this is also where problems in today's workplace are solved.

In their book *Leading with Heart*, Baird and Sullivan (2022) revealed five behaviors that all transformative leaders engage in, which allow them to connect authentically with their teams. At the top of this list is being aware of the needs of their employees (p. 9). What Bloom discovered many years ago is now confirmed in the research conducted by Baird and Sullivan in that people who are engaged on a deep personal and human level interact with positive emotions that are indicative of critical thinking skills, leading to positive results.

Blanchard and Hodges (2005) differentiated between life role leadership and organizational leadership. Organizational leadership is typified by activities that lead to organizational success and is grounded in relationships that are based on power, rewards, material consequences, and recognition (p. 9). Alternatively, life role leadership focuses on the growth and development of people and "functions in enduring relationships" (p. 8). In stark contrast to popular leadership models today, the authors offer the following advice: "Leaders, seeking to grow and develop people as an end goal of equal importance to results, need a healthy capacity to forgive, correct, and move on" (Blanchard & Hodges, 2005, p. 76).

The ability to forgive and move on does not come naturally for most people. Transformed, people-focused leaders are aware of this tendency, and they strive to always understand that making a mistake can happen to anybody—especially themselves. In his first foray as a ship commander, Chester Nimitz ran aground in shallow water and got the vessel he oversaw stuck in the mud. Several hours elapsed while Nimitz and his crew waited for another ship to come and set them free from their predicament. Although he was court-martialed and reprimanded for neglect of duty, Nimitz never forgot about this incident when the need arose to discipline his subordinates after he had ascended to Commander in Chief of the Pacific Fleet for the United States in World War II (Potter, 2013).

Humility is an additional characteristic of leaders seeking to transform their organization through quality, purpose-driven relationships. In explaining the difference between good leaders and great leaders, Collins (2001) specifically mentions the difference humility makes as leaders lead their organizations. Collins stipulates that "Level 5" or great leaders are "a study in duality: modest and willful, humble and fearless" (p. 22). Collins also goes on to explain that whereas "Level 4" or good leaders may possess a great personality, "Level 5" leaders maintain the ability to produce a great program via dedicated humility (p. 27) because they realize that no one person is the expert at everything that is going on within an organization. In other words, there is no "I" in the word "team." The transformed leader serves to meet the needs of others with an attitude of meekness that is attractive to others. People are influenced by leaders who are sensitive to them and who genuinely care about helping them, either on a personal or professional level.

Lastly, relationship building is a process that requires time and patience. Culver (2009) indicated that leadership develops through maturation: "If maturation in a skill was not necessary, the genius Mozart would have written *The Marriage of Figaro* at age 12 instead of 30" (p. 5). It is the same with building relationships. Truly wise, prudent leaders are people who genuinely understand the importance of shared leadership. Shared leadership will ultimately depend on the quality of relationships that have developed over time. As a result, transformed leaders are those who have matured to the point that they realize time spent building meaningful relationships is critically important to not only their success but the success of their organization as well.

CASE STUDY

After spending eight years as a classroom teacher, the most recent adjustment to your career path has taken a more upwardly mobile turn in the direction of school administration. Now in your second year as the principal of a small school (300 students at your campus), you completely understand the notion that "doing the right thing is not always easy and doing the easy thing is not always right." Although your online master's degree was well worth the amount of money you invested, you find yourself wondering if the activities, coursework, and instructors had nary a clue about the real-life situation that has descended upon you with the weight of what feels like a 747 that has both taken off and landed right in the middle of your mind.

For starters, a younger student at the campus you lead (grades 6–8) has complained about not getting enough sleep at night. This student has been sent to your office due to a minor discipline matter and for not following directions. The social worker in you is wondering if the two concerns are related while the school administrator in you is screaming to "get this kid back to class as quickly as possible" so you can move on to the umpteen other matters that popped up on your to-do list just this morning.

Not sure about what to do, you decide to do what a lot of people do in these situations—you stall for time. You proceed to tell the student in question to remain in your office while you take a stroll down the hall as if you are going to be dealing with some official school business. So you leave the door open that leads to the foyer where your secretary works and you head out the back door, which opens to the aforementioned hallway.

On your journey, you pass by a restroom and overhear one student tell another student, "That _____ is gonna get what's coming to her!" Your senses now on hyperalert, you begin to eavesdrop on the conversation and discover they are talking about one of your teachers. Furthermore, you learn they are planning to inflict bodily harm on this individual and do it in such a way that nobody will suspect it was them.

Now, to be honest, the teacher these students are referring to can at times be difficult, but she definitely doesn't deserve what they are planning to do. You get closer to the entrance of the bathroom door (the students are the opposite gender as you) in an attempt to see if you can identify who these students are. The closer you get, the louder their voices become, and you think this is going to be easy, when in a moment's notice, you hear several loud bangs almost simultaneously. Scared to death that what you have just heard is gunfire, you start running in the direction of the loud bangs.

As best you can tell, the sounds were coming from behind a door that leads outside to a parking lot that is adjacent to the cafeteria on your campus. With the caution of a policeman, you start to open the door only to realize that if you do, whoever is doing the shooting may just open up on you. Not really sure that you are doing the right thing, you proceed to open the door anyway and find a tremendous amount of wrappings from numerous Black Cat firecrackers that have just exploded.

To make matters worse, two of your best teachers—fine educators both, who have a long history of extremely high evaluations that you yourself have awarded—are laughing uncontrollably at the sight before their very eyes. At that moment, you realize that it is Friday, April 1st and you are probably never going to live this down. Realizing that you've got "bigger fish to fry" back in the restroom, you spin on your heels to return to the area where all this started, only to find the students now gone and pandemonium has engulfed your campus.

For the next hour, it is almost impossible to get things to return to normal. The superintendent and several school board members have called to assure you of their support. You've already sent out instant messages on the numerous technological devices that allow you to do so and explained that the event was related to a practical joke instigated by two very well-respected employees, both of whom are about to retire.

After lunch, your mind returns to the two competing concerns that you had when all this started: the young student who was sent to your office and the two students you overheard in the bathroom, threatening to injure someone. What do you do next?

It's now 1:30 p.m., and school will end at 3:30 p.m. You've got two hours to formulate a plan and hopefully resolve both issues. At your disposal is an assistant principal and a guidance counselor, both of whom are extremely busy with issues of their own.

DISCUSSION QUESTIONS

1. In light of what has been discussed in this chapter, set a course of action and explain which of these issues are most important in your view.
2. Which situation is more pressing and will require your personal intervention? Or do they both require you to be personally involved?
3. Do you have enough time to do what you are planning to do? Please explain your thoughts.
4. How would you listen and display empathy, all the while maintaining a level of professionalism and courtesy that others not only respect but adopt as a way of dealing with this type of stressful dilemma themselves?

Certainly, there are some individuals that are in need of a "stern warning" about their actions because their behavior could have resulted in dire consequences. Is there a consideration about timing here—maybe delaying your actions until you are sure you have your emotions in check prior to addressing a concern? Please articulate your response against the backdrop of what you have read in this chapter.

REFERENCES

Abdullahi, A. Z., Anarfo, E. B., & Anyigba, H. (2020). The impact of leadership style on organizational citizenship behavior: Does leaders' emotional intelligence play a moderating role? *Journal of Management Development, 39*(9/10), 963–987.

Anderson, A. (n.d.). *12 Remote work statistics to know in 2022.* NorthOne. Retrieved October 12, 2022, from https://www.northone.com/blog/small-business/remote-work-statistics

Baird, J., & Sullivan, E. (2022). *Leading with heart: Five conversations that unlock creativity, purpose, and results.* HarperCollins.

Blanchard, K., and Hodges, P. (2005). *Lead like Jesus.* Thomas Nelson.

Bloom, B. (1956). *Taxonomy of educational objectives. Handbook I: The cognitive domain.* David McKay.

Bramlett, C. H. (2018). *Servant leadership roadmap: Master the 12 core competencies of management success with leadership qualities and interpersonal skills.* CreateSpace.

Buckingham, M., and Coffman, C. (1999). *First break all the rules.* Simon & Schuster.

Chaudhary, P., Rohtagi, M., Singh, R. K., & Arora, S. (2022). Impact of leader's e-competencies on employees' wellbeing in global virtual teams during COVID-19: The moderating role of emotional intelligence. *Employee Relations: The International Journal, 44*(5), 1048–1063.

Chernow, R. (1998). *Titan: The life of John D. Rockefeller, Sr.* Random House.

Collins, J. C. (2001). *Good to great: Why some companies make the leap . . . and others don't.* HarperCollins.

Conner, D. R. (1992). *Managing at the speed of change: How resilient managers succeed and prosper where others fail.* Villard.

Connors, C. D. (2021). *Emotional intelligence for the modern leader: A guide to cultivating effective leadership and organizations.* Rockridge Press.

Covey, S. M. (2022). *Trust and inspire: How truly great leaders unleash greatness in others.* Simon & Schuster.

Culver, M. K. (2009). *Applying servant leadership in today's schools.* Routledge.

Dåderman, A. M., Ronthy, M., Ekegren, M., & Mårdberg, B. E. (2013). "Managing with my heart, brain, and soul": The development of the leadership intelligence questionnaire. *Journal of Cooperative Education and Internships, 47*(1), 61–77.

Davidson, J. P. (1989). *The marketing sourcebook for small business.* Wiley and Sons.

Fix, R. L., & Atnafou-Boyer, R. (2022). Assessing the impact and effectiveness of a community leadership development program on black leaders. *Journal of Leadership Education, 21*(1), 32–50.

Ghalavi, Z., & Nastiezaie, N. (2020). Relationship of servant leadership and organizational citizenship behavior with mediation of psychological empowerment.
Eurasian Journal of Educational Research, 89(2), 241–264.

Gillis, A. S. (2022, January). *What is an exabyte?* TechTarget. https://www.techtarget
.com/searchstorage/definition/exabyte

Goleman, D. (1998). *Working with emotional intelligence.* Bantam Books.

Gómez-Leal, R., Holzer, A. A., Bradley, C., Fernández-Berrocal, P., & Patti, J. (2022).
The relationship between emotional intelligence and leadership in school leaders: A
systematic review. *Cambridge Journal of Education, 52*(1), 1–21.

Goodlet, K. J., Raney, E., Buckley, K., Afolabi, T., Davis, L., Fettkether, R. M.,
Jones, M., Larson, S., & Tennant, S. (2022). Impact of the COVID-19 pandemic
on the emotional intelligence of student pharmacist leaders. *American Journal of
Pharmaceutical Education, 86*(1), 32–36.

Greenleaf, R. K. (1977). *The servant as leader.* Robert Greenleaf Center.

Greenleaf, R. K. (1991). *The servant as leader.* Greenleaf Center for Servant
Leadership.

Harms, P. D., & Credé, M. (2010). Emotional intelligence and transformational and
transactional leadership: A meta-analysis. *Journal of Leadership and Organization
Studies, 17*(1), 5–17.

Kaur, N., & Hirudayaraj, M. (2021). The role of leader emotional intelligence in
organizational learning: A literature review using 4I framework. *New Horizons in
Adult Education & Human Resources Development, 33*(1), 51–68.

Kearney, W. S., Kelsey, C., & Sinkfield, C. (2014). Emotionally intelligent leadership:
An analysis of targeted interventions for aspiring school leaders in Texas. *Planning
and Changing, 45*(1/2), 31–47.

Kiker, D. S., Callahan, J. S., & Kiker, M. B. (2019). Exploring the boundaries of
servant leadership: A meta-analysis of the main and moderating effects of servant
leadership on behavioral and affective outcomes. *Journal of Managerial Issues,
31*(2), 172–197.

Kim, T., You, Y., & Hong, J. (2021). A study on the relationship among servant
leadership, authentic leadership, perceived organizational support (POS) and agile
culture using PLS-SEM: Mediating effect of POS. *Elementary Education Online,
20*(1), 784–795.

Kriegel, R., & Brandt, D. (1996). *Sacred cows make the best burgers: Developing
change-ready people and organizations.* Warner Books.

Labby, S., Lunenburg, F. C., & Slate, J. R. (2013). Emotional intelligence skills and
principal characteristics. *Journal of Educational Research, 7*(4), 257–268.

Lodestar Solutions. (n.d.). *How fast is knowledge doubling?* Retrieved October
12, 2022, from https://lodestarsolutions.com/keeping-up-with-the-surge-of
-information-and-human-knowledge/

Mayer, J. D., & Salovey, P. (1997). What is emotional intelligence? In P. Salovey &
D. J. Sluyter (Eds.), *Emotional development and emotional intelligence* (pp. 3–31).
Basic Books.

Nelson, D. B., & Low, G. R. (2011). *Emotional intelligence* (2nd ed.). Prentice Hall.

Parrish, D. R. (2015). The relevance of emotional intelligence for leadership in a higher education context. *Studies in Higher Education, 40*(5), 821–837.

Potter, E. B. (2013). *Nimitz.* Naval Institute Press.

Salovey P., & Mayer, J. D. (1990). Emotional intelligence. *Imagination, Cognition and Personality, 9*(3), 185–211.

Scott, S. (2004). *Fierce conversations: Achieving success at work and in life, one conversation at a time.* Berkley.

Searchquotes (n.d.). John C. Maxwell Leadership Quotes. Retrieved from https://www.searchquotes.com/quotation/Competence_goes_beyond_words._It%27s_the_leader%27s_ability_to_say_it%2C_plan_it%2C_and_do_it_in_such_a_way_/29449/

Silsbee, L. (2015, May 18). *The top 7 challenges facing leaders today.* LinkedIn. https://www.linkedin.com/pulse/top-7-challenges-facing-leaders-today-lynda-silsbee-cpt-sphr/

Wallace, J., Blackhourn, J. M., Giesler, B., & Hylen, M. (2022). Servant leadership: Basic propositions. *Kentucky Journal of Excellence in College Teaching and Learning, 18*(1), 68–76.

Wirawan, H. K., Tamar, M., & Bellani, E. (2018). Principals' leadership styles: The role of emotional intelligence and achievement motivation. *International Journal of Education Management, 33*(5), 1094–1105.

Wittmer, J. L. S., & Hopkins, M. M. (2021). Leading remotely in a time of crisis: Relationships with emotional intelligence. *Journal of Leadership & Organizational Studies, 29*(2), 176–189.

Yukl, G., & Mahsud, R. (2010). Why flexible and adaptive leadership is essential. *Consulting Psychology Journal: Practice and Research, 62*(2), 81–93.

Ziglar, Z. (2000). *See you at the top: 25th Anniversary edition.* Pelican.

Chapter 5

Peopled Leadership and Building Community

Putting It All Together

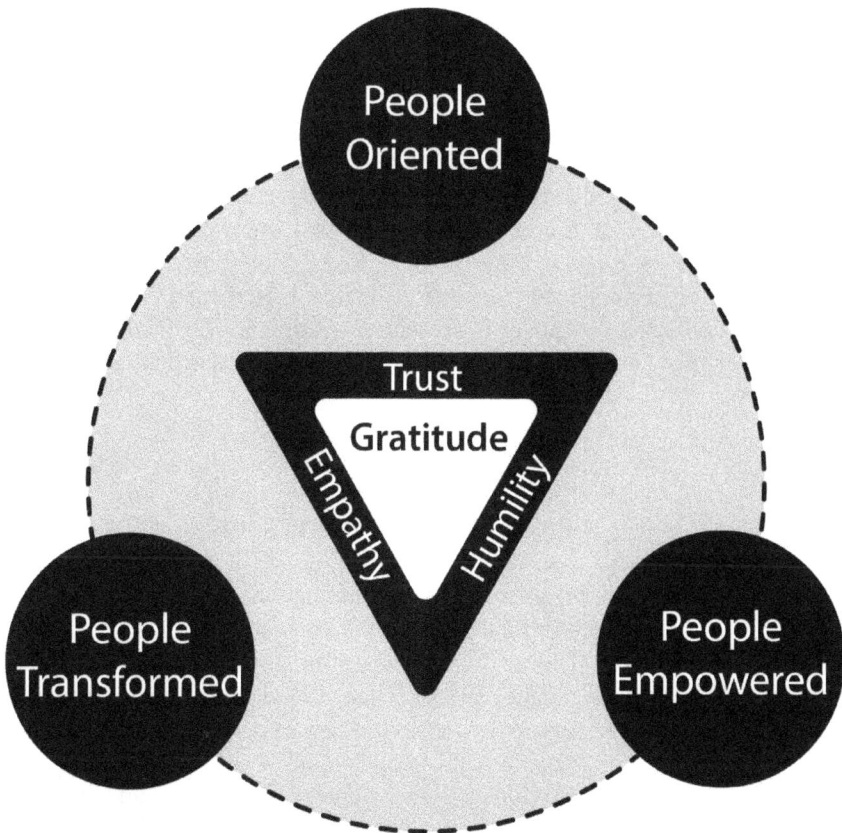

Fig. 5.1. *Peopled Leadership*: The Practice of Gratitude. *Jack Ousey.*

It is critical for 21st-century leaders to have strategies that align resources, people, and plans with needed organizational outcomes. For leaders to successfully address the challenges in today's workplace, they need a new approach that generates deep levels of trust and builds relationships that help sustain and transform organization members into a team that can be successful in the tumultuous currents of the 21st century. True leaders act with the whole person (physical, social, mental, emotional, and spiritual) in mind, understanding the interconnected nature of these different facets of the individual. Covey (2022) promotes a "people centered approach" he calls "trust and inspire" (p. 24). This approach, according to Covey, "enables us to build teams, collaborate, and innovate. And it's what attracts and engages today's top talent" (p. 24).

The *Peopled Leadership* model is a more comprehensive model that provides strategies at each phase of the development of the organization and its members through which leaders can build trust, provide resources, and continue to nurture the well-being of the members of the organization, all while keeping an eye on the needed outcomes. To this approach, we add the ingredient that sets the *Peopled Leadership* model apart: an attitude of gratitude.

Twenty-first-century workplaces need *peopled leaders*, leaders who focus on the people and their well-being first. By focusing on the well-being of people, the organization has the ability to grow. Adler's (1956) work provides a baseline for understanding the nature and importance of community. Maslow's hierarchy of needs when overlaid with the *Peopled Leadership* model, provides a road map for how to build community and empower an organization. Finally, the secret and unique ingredient that undergirds the *Peopled Leadership* model is presented: gratitude. The final section of this chapter provides a case study that illustrates how the theory connects to practice.

THE NEED FOR BELONGING AND
SENSE OF COMMUNITY

In the early 20th century, Adler (1956) studied the human need for community and belonging. He referred to this need as *Gemeinschaftsgefühl*, literally translated, "community feeling." Couched against the backdrop of humans' need for affection, Adler believed that when people's need for community and belonging is not being met by those organizations to which they belong, they turn inward and away from the organization. Community feeling can facilitate collaboration, provide support in times of difficulty, and improve efficiency. However, Adler warns that the notion of community feeling can be abused. Adler posits that community "must be thought of as everlasting, as we could think of it if mankind had reached the goal of perfection" (p. 142). In practical terms, a feeling of community is always in the process of becoming. It is something a 21st-century leader must be constantly nourishing.

The entirety of the *Peopled Leadership* model was created to support the need to build a sense of community within the organization. As leaders continuously work to nurture a feeling of community, they should not lose sight of the role of each individual in forming and maintaining that community. Adler (1956) admonishes, "All great achievements of humanity originate in the social genius of individuals" (p. 450). By building trust with individual members, trust can also be built within and across the organization. A sense of community is an important step toward creating a transformed organization. The collaboration that becomes possible in a transformed organization creates the synergy necessary for such essential processes as creative problem solving, critical thinking, and teamwork.

Despite all of the potential benefits of community, Adler (1956) provides one note of caution. As with any human enterprise, there is the potential for exploitation and abuse: "Pretense of social interest . . . like a veil, covers other tendencies. These tendencies must be uncovered to arrive at a correct evaluation" (p. 140). Peopled leaders understand Adler's belief that "All great achievements of humanity originate in the social genius of individuals," and they use the skills embedded in *Peopled Leadership*. Such a leader has the ability to become "a real human being who possesses courage and skills" and "becomes realized what others . . . dream about" (Adler, 1956, p. 450).

MASLOW'S MOTIVATION THEORY AND *PEOPLED LEADERSHIP*

For many years, preservice teachers have learned about motivating students for learning. The keystone for many has been Maslow's Hierarchy of Needs. First published in 1943, Maslow's hierarchy postulates that the basic human needs, physiological, safety, belonging, and esteem, must be met prior to meeting any more advanced needs. According to Maslow (1943), "Human needs arrange themselves in hierarchies of prepotency. The appearance of one usually rests on the prior satisfaction of another, more prepotent need" (p. 370). More importantly for leaders, Maslow (1943) points out, "no need or drive can be treated as if it were isolated or discrete; every drive is related to the state of satisfaction or dissatisfaction of other drives" (p. 370). Further, Maslow also states that when basic needs are not met, people become fixed on those needs until they are met, precluding the possibility of any effort to address other needs. Table 5.1 shows the correlation between Maslow's hierarchy of needs and the *Peopled Leadership* model.

Table 5.1 Maslow's Theory of Motivation Applied to *Peopled Leadership*

Maslow (1943) Needs	Peopled Leadership Phase	Description
Transcendence Self-Actualization	People Transformed	As members see their individual potential being realized, they see the organization's potential being realized as well. Members and the organization begin to see even greater potential, individually and collectively.
Aesthetic Needs Cognitive Needs	People Empowered	With trust established, members begin to make decisions about their own professional learning. They seek out needed resources. Members discover meaning in their own work and what their work means in the context of the organization. The beauty of the organization's ability to function at a high level further empowers members to increase their autonomy while remaining focused on the organization's goals.
Esteem Needs Belonging/Love Needs Safety Needs Physiological Needs	People Oriented	The organization works on building trust. As trust is established and then maintained, members begin to feel a sense of safety and belonging. Members are able to be more open to one another, which leads to goals being accomplished and a feeling of value in individuals and the organization. This leads to a raised level of esteem, individually and collectively.

The most basic need within an organization is trust. Trust starts with leaders since it is prerequisite to being a leader. Trust is a pattern of consistent, predictive, and positive behaviors that promote intended outcomes and create a sense of safety, belonging, and esteem within and between members of a group. The main focus of the People Oriented phase of the model is building a foundation of trust on which the organization's functioning and output can be based. However, peopled leaders understand that building and maintaining trust are both ongoing processes. Until members of the organization feel safe in the work environment, it is unlikely they will be able to take the calculated risks necessary for personal professional growth as well as to facilitate the growth and productivity of the organization.

As safety levels increase in individuals, their sense of identity as part of the organization increases and becomes embedded in their interactions with colleagues and external stakeholders, in their work product, and in their attitudes. When the quality of workplace environment and product improves, the esteem levels of those in the organization tend to increase as well. The leader can then begin to shift focus from establishing trust to maintaining trust. Members of the organization then begin to feel the freedom to become decision-makers concerning their individual professional goals. The transition to phase two, People Empowered, has begun.

Once the organization has begun to transition from a focus on establishing trust to maintaining trust, members of the organization have seen their most basic professional needs met. They feel safe within the organization and gain clarity about their role in helping the organization achieve needed outcomes. In turn, this sense of belonging helps organization members experience an enhanced level of self-esteem, both individually seeing their role in the organization's success and increased esteem in the overall health of the organization itself. Members are now positioned to make decisions that affect both their individual work and the work of the organization. The leader has become what Wiseman (2017) refers to has a *multiplier*.

Wiseman believes multipliers are leaders who:

> have a rich view of the intelligence of the people around them. They don't see a world where just a few people deserve to do the thinking. [They see] intelligence as continually developing. . . . They assume people are smart. To their eyes, their organization is full of talented people who are capable of contributing at much higher levels. (p. 19)

Multipliers are leaders who develop, challenge, and consult members of the organization. These behaviors provide the support required for members of the organization to have the freedom to become decision-makers and by extension, risk-takers. These behaviors are only possible with the deep levels of trust established in the People Oriented phase of our model. The stage has now been set for members of the organization to experience self-actualization and transcendence, ushering in the final phase of our model, People (and by extension, the organization) Transformed.

In 1943, Maslow identified self-actualization as the pinnacle human need. Self-actualization was defined as "the desire to become more and more what one is, to become everything that one is capable of becoming" (p. 382). Peopled leaders understand that self-actualization will vary from member to member, depending on the talent, skills, goals, and needs of the individual. It is the peopled leader's responsibility to discover how best to meet the needs of each member within the context and needs of the organization and make the needed resources and opportunities available to each.

Late in Maslow's life and career, he came to believe his original theory of needs and motivation was not complete and added a new capstone, self-transcendence. Self-transcendence is also the key characteristic of the third and final phase of the *Peopled Leadership* model, People Transformed. Maslow (1969) believed that as people achieve transcendence, they transition from focusing on the realization of personal potential to looking beyond themselves to the potential of others, particularly those with whom they are associated. Koltko-Rivera (2006) asserts that those who have attained transcendence "seek to further a cause beyond the self and . . . experience a communion beyond the boundaries of the self through peak experience" (p. 303). When members of the organization shift their orientation from self to others, peopled leaders know the organization has reached the third and final phase of the *Peopled Leadership* model.

Organizations comprised of transcendent members are teams that work together like a fine-tuned watch. They seek out each other's talents and skills to achieve both individual and team goals. The peopled leader unleashes the intelligence, talents, expertise, and desire of the organization's members to release the potential of the team. Skills such as planning, problem solving, and risk-taking and high levels of motivation have become second nature.

PEOPLED LEADERSHIP AND GOLDSTEIN'S HOLISTIC VIEW OF SELF-ACTUALIZATION

Goldstein (1963a) provided further emphasis to Maslow's original work by concluding that self-actualization is the principal force that drives the motivation and decision-making of individuals: "The tendency to actualize itself is the motive which sets the organism going: it is the *drive* by which the organism is moved" (p. 140). Goldstein parted ways with Maslow in terms of the relationship between individuals and their environment, thus the notion of holism, the belief that one cannot completely understand an individual apart from understanding the environment in which the individual operates:

> The essence of the organism is brought into actualization through the environmental changes that act upon it. The expressions of this actualization are the performances of the organism. Through them the organism can deal with the respective environmental demands and actualize itself. (Goldstein, 1963b, pp. 111–112)

Goldstein's work has two major implications for peopled leaders: to understand the drive of their members provided by their need to achieve self-actualization and the importance of understanding members' environments in order to understand them. In essence, the peopled leader must be aware of the totality of each team member.

In today's world, many forces affect the ability of individuals to perform at high levels and thus contribute to the success of the organization. The forces include providing for one and one's family physically, financially, emotionally, socially, emotionally, and spiritually. These forces require the peopled leader to maintain an awareness of each member holistically. Peopled leaders use this awareness to provide the resources necessary to meet these various needs in the organization's members. By meeting members' individual needs, many of the needs of the organization are also being met. The foundation of meeting these needs is the continuous belief in the value of each member. The secret ingredient for valuing members of the organization is maintaining an attitude of gratitude.

THE SECRET INGREDIENT: THE PRACTICE OF GRATITUDE

Many leadership models are comprised of similar elements. Some of the more common elements are trust (Bartell & Bartell, 2016; Covey, 2022; Zenger & Folkman, 2009), relationship building (Kelley, 2018), and collaboration (Cameron & Quinn, 2011; Hersey, 1984). These elements have been presented as part of the *Peopled Leadership* model. However, there is an additional element that sets the *Peopled Leadership* model apart from all others. The *Peopled Leadership* model features the practice of gratitude. A relatively recent area of emphasis in research, the importance of gratitude in leadership is just now coming into focus.

Research Concerning Gratitude

The word *gratitude* is derived from the Latin word *gratus*, which means pleasing, welcome, or agreeable. From this same Latin root comes words such as *grace* and *gratis*. According to Emmons and Stern (2013), all derivatives from *gratus* "have to do with kindness, generousity, gifts, the beauty of giving and receiving" (p. 846). They believe feelings of gratitude are "anchored in two essential pieces of information processed by an individual: an affirming of goodness or 'good things' in one's life and the recognition that the sources of this goodness lie at least partially outside the self" (pp. 846–847).

McGuire et al. (2019) identified two different types of gratitude: trait gratitude and state gratitude. Trait gratitude is defined as "the predisposition to be aware of situations in which one receives benefits from others and represents between-person differences in the threshold to experience gratitude, without reference to context" (p. 2250). State gratitude is "a discrete experience that occurs when one perceives themselves as the recipient of a positive outcome, triggering a subsequent desire to reciprocate" (p. 2250). Trait gratitude is a trait, whereas state gratitude is an action. McGuire et al. concluded that the active participation in gratitude (state gratitude) contributes to a health-related high quality of life, whereas trait gratitude does not.

Healthy, growing organizations are organizations that promote continuous professional learning. New technologies, new relationships, new products, and new ideas all require a focus on learning for members of the organization. In a 2016 study on the effects of an attitude of gratitude on learning, Wilson (2016) asserts that "gratitude shows significant benefits to a person's overall well-being and ability to flourish in life psychologically, spiritually, and physically" (p. 1). Results of this study indicate that learners who were reminded to practice gratitude "experienced greater benefits for focus and resilience in learning" (p. 1). Results of Wilson's study also indicate the practice of gratitude can contribute to having a calmer and more positive outlook, lessening stress, and increasing focus for facing challenges.

A significant and profound measure of the impact of gratitude on a person's well-being was reported in the work of Jans-Beken and Wong (2021), who developed an instrument for measuring the impact of dispositional gratitude and existential gratitude on the spiritual well-being of individuals. Dispositional gratitude is defined as "the tendency to feel grateful for the positive things in life," whereas existential gratitude is the ability to "count blessings in both good times and times of suffering" (p. 73). Results of this study demonstrate existential gratitude was associated with a strong sense of spiritual well-being. This indicates that a deep sense of gratitude, even in the tough times, is a key element to maintaining a positive outlook and having a sense of hope for the future.

The increased sense of spiritual well-being identified by Jans-Beken and Wong (2021) provides additional support for the work of Algoe (2012), which identified a relationship between gratitude and self-care. Algoe concluded the belief in the positive motivation for others' kind actions is an important condition to be able to experience gratitude. Bartlett et al. (2020) go a step further. They sought to discover if there was a relationship between power and gratitude. They define power as "control over resources (e.g., money, status, decision-making) due to differential social standing" (p. 27). Bartlett et al.'s research indicates a strong relationship between self-care, high levels of self-esteem, and gratitude. The authors state, "To our knowledge, this is the first research to find a positive relationship between power and gratitude and to offer self-esteem as one mechanism for this relationship" (p. 35).

A growing body of research has examined whether or not gratitude has an effect on relationship building and maintenance (Algoe, 2012; Algoe et al.,

2008; Gu et al., 2022). Considering the central nature of relationship building to the *Peopled Leadership* model and that most people spend at least 33% of their lives in the workplace, looking for possible applications of this body of research to the demands of 21st-century leadership seems wise. Evidence that gratitude is an effective tool for building and maintaining relationships would provide substantial support for the effectiveness of the *Peopled Leadership* model.

In 2008, Algoe et al. provided the first empirical evidence that gratitude is an effective tool for building and maintaining relationships. The results of their study indicate that gratitude is effective as a relationship builder in both dyadic (between two people) and group situations. Applied to leadership, this result provides evidence that gratitude is an effective leadership tool whether used with individual members of an organization or with the organization itself. This study describes the benefits of gratitude in building relationships as "a detection-and-response system to help find, remind, and bind ourselves to attentive others" (p. 429).

Algoe and Haidt (2009) examined the nature of "other praising" emotions in social interactions. These emotions are elevation, gratitude, and admiration. Elevation is defined as the "feeling that one has been uplifted . . . in some way" due to "acts of charity, gratitude, fidelity, generosity, or any other strong display of virtue" (p. 106). Further, elevation can result in physical or emotional feelings. Gratitude is "triggered by the perception that one is the beneficiary of another's intentionally-provided benefit" (p. 106). Admiration is defined as "what people feel when they see extraordinary displays of skill, talent, or achievement" (p. 107).

Results of this study indicate gratitude leads organization members to have a "desire to repay and acknowledge others' actions, which may serve to enhance a relationship with the other person" (Algoe & Haidt, 2009, p. 112). In addition, this study found evidence that grateful individuals tend to be more focused on giving to others and the emotions of elevation, gratitude, and admiration tend to contribute to the enrichment of both relationship with oneself (intrapersonal development) and relationships with others (interpersonal development). The researchers concluded that of the three, gratitude provided the most robust body of evidence of increasing the desire for organization members to feel closer to one another (Algoe & Haidt, 2009).

In 2012, Algoe further clarified the work of Algoe et al. (2008) that established the "find, remind, and bind" theory of gratitude. A theory that helps explain the benefits of gratitude, Algoe (2012) asserts that find, remind, and bind

> posits that rather than primarily helping us understand how we might come to trust a stranger, gratitude is probably best understood as a mechanism for

forming and sustaining the most *important* [emphasis in the original] relationships of our lives, those with the people we care about and count on from one
day to the next. (p. 456)

Find, remind, and bind means gratitude serves to "improve the relationship:
that is, it *finds* new or *reminds* of a known good relationship partner, and
helps to *bind* recipient and benefactor closer together" (Algoe, 2012, p. 457).

   In a recently published study, Gu, Ocampo, Algoe, and Oveis (2022) used
an experimental approach to investigate the possible effects of gratitude
on how people respond physiologically to stress. Participants included 200
undergraduate students (100 dyads) from a university in California. The
dyads were either roommates or suite mates for at least four months. Findings
from this study include the following:

1. Gratitude buffers against biological threat responses during teamwork.
2. Gratitude enhanced cardiovascular efficiency. (p. 8)

   These results are important in that they provide empirical evidence that
gratitude helps reduce stress, which can lead to enhanced cardiovascular health.

Benefits of Gratitude

From the above review of the research on gratitude, the following themes have
emerged: (1) Gratitude is related to well-being and increased self-esteem, (2)
gratitude that is active (existential gratitude, state gratitude) is a powerful
tool for affecting the well-being of team members as opposed to nonactive
types of gratitude (trait gratitude, dispositional gratitude), and (3) the effects
of gratitude are evidenced across multiple facets of both the organization
and the individuals who comprise it. These themes hold potentially powerful
implications for leadership in the tumultuous 21st century.

   The practice of sincere gratitude within organizations is key to establishing and maintaining trust, the core of the People Oriented phase of *Peopled
Leadership*. Actively expressing gratitude reminds team members that they
are trusted and valued. In organizations where gratitude is practiced, it
becomes a fundamental element of a positive, systemic culture. Gratitude also
leads to an improved sense of psychological, sociological, and physiological well-being. These are keys to empowering members of the organization,
the focus on the second phase of *Peopled Leadership*, People Empowered.
Lastly, there is empirical evidence that gratitude leads to improved relationships between individuals within teams and across the teams themselves.
Improved relationships, built on trust and cemented with gratitude, lead to

team members and the team itself being transformed, phase three of *Peopled Leadership*.

Leading With an Attitude of Gratitude

The major question of this section is, why is gratitude central to successful leadership? The *Peopled Leadership* model is based on the belief that treating people well, valuing them and their work, and meeting the needs of the whole individual are what true leaders are called to do. Gratitude is the glue that binds together the relationships that are critical to successful leadership. This view of leadership is consistent with Greenleaf's (1977) notion of servant leadership in which the servant leader "make[s] sure other people's highest priority needs are being met" so those in the organization "become healthier, wiser, freer, more autonomous, more likely themselves to become servants" (p. 27).

People-Oriented Phase and Gratitude

People Oriented as a phase of *Peopled Leadership* has a twofold meaning: a beginning point and the focus of the leader's efforts in team building and culture development. When a person becomes a leader of an organization, the first step to establishing oneself as the leader is to establish a culture of trust. Gratitude plays a key role in this effort. Gratitude communicates to the members they are valued by the leader. As other members of the organization pick up the pattern of expressing gratitude from the leader, a culture of mutual support and caring begins to develop because members feel valued as individuals. Valued individuals who trust the organization's leader become more willing to invest themselves in reaching the group's desired outcomes. As a result, the organization becomes a team with the synergy and cohesiveness to meet individual and team challenges and solve problems as they arise. In Greenleaf's (1977) words, organization members become servants to each other and to outside stakeholders.

Gratitude is also a key element in keeping the leader focused on the people in the organization, their individual goals, needs, and desires. When the leader expresses gratitude to individuals within the organization, they are reminded they have value and that their value has been noticed (the leader sees their value) and recognized (the leader expresses it, so the team members know the leader knows). For example, at a church staff meeting a few years ago, the senior minister of a large church spent most of the meeting acknowledging each member of the staff by identifying a specific gift or talent he saw in that staff member and the value that gift brought to the staff and the church and expressing gratitude for that person and that person's gift. This experience resulted in deeper levels of trust, greater cohesiveness among the staff, and a stronger commitment from each staff member to the church and its programs. Jans-Beken and Wong's (2021) work provides empirical evidence of these benefits of gratitude.

People-Empowered Phase and Gratitude

The People Empowered phase of *Peopled Leadership* refers to the growing autonomy of the members of the organization that occurs as trust begins to result in the establishment and maintenance of healthy, growing relationships between team members and between each team member and the leader. The work of Algoe (2012) and Gu et al. (2022) suggests that the consistent, sincere use of gratitude provides much of the needed underpinning for these relationships to form. As the work of Gu et al. (2022) points out, the practicing of being grateful for one's organization members has positive effects on their physiological, psychological, and sociological well-being. They feel safe in the organization, safe to be themselves and safe to take calculated risks in their work to help the organization reach its intended outcomes. This sense of well-being and safety in the organization provides the foundation for increased autonomy. Trust, combined with autonomy, leads to empowerment.

Autonomy refers to the ability of team members to make decisions about their goals, work, and professional needs. Empowerment is when the leader steps back to allow team members to become decision-makers about their work. Gratitude helps the leader create the conditions with the team so its members have the overall health and ability to be empowered.

People-Transformed Phase and Gratitude

People Transformed occurs as members of the organization begin to use their autonomy and ability as decision-makers to look beyond themselves for the benefit of the organization. People Transformed is manifested in synergy and collaboration becoming second nature to the organization. This culture is encapsulated in Algoe et al.'s (2008) "find, remind, and bind" theory of gratitude. Gratitude creates a cycle through which relationships are continuously renewed through the reemphasis of each team member's worth and value, both individually and to the organization.

Transformed organizations also create a culture in which the well-being of each member is a top priority. The attitude and practice of gratitude can support improved physical health (Gu et al., 2022), emotional health (Algoe & Haidt, 2009), and spiritual health (Jans-Beken & Wong, 2021). As the health and well-being of individual members improve, so do the health and well-being of the organization. Author Amy Weatherly once wrote:

Some people could be given an entire field of roses and only see the thorns in it. Others could be given a single weed and only see the wildflower in it. Perception is a key component to gratitude. And gratitude is a key component of joy. (as cited in Dewar, 2021)

Gratitude provides the foundation for a culture of well-being, collaboration, and joy. In practice, it is the responsibility of the leader to maintain an attitude of gratitude to continue nurturing the practices that have transformed the organization and its members.

SUMMARY: BRIDGING THEORY TO PRACTICE

Workplaces need *peopled leaders*, leaders who focus on the people and their well-being first. Building trust leads to stronger relationships, autonomous and motivated team members, and transformed team members and a transformed organization. How does a 21st-century leader lead with an attitude of gratitude? In this section, we discuss some practices to help connect the theory with the reality of the challenges in today's workplace.

Practice 1: Make a habit out of saying thank-you in a variety of ways. Today's communication is done rapidly to address challenges in real time. The constant bombardment of emails and text messages alone keeps the average worker busy, and leaders can become inundated with communications to return. Adding the word *thanks* to a return text or email can make a huge difference in the culture of the organization. This practice reminds team members they are valued for who they are and the skill set they bring to the team. Communicating gratitude, whether verbally, through a text, or in an email, confirms team members' worth in real time. This practice also communicates to team members that the leader is always working to build and maintain the kind of culture in which trust can be built and then maintained.

Practice 2: Look for concrete ways to show gratitude. Something as simple as a handwritten thank-you note, particularly in the current age of technology, can be meaningful. It shows thought and the expenditure of the leader's time to show gratitude. In chapters 3 and 4, the need for properly resourcing one's people was discussed. Once trust is established, team members can be depending on helping the leader accurately identify needed resources and then use those resources wisely. Whenever possible, going beyond the basics when possible is an effective way to express gratitude. For example, higher education faculty must be able to travel to make presentations or give performances that are required for promotion and tenure. Most universities provide a basic level of funding to offset some of those costs. Finding additional resources to minimize the cost that comes out of the faculty member's pocket is an effective way to nurture trust and express gratitude. Providing a celebratory meal is also an effective way to show gratitude.

Practice 3: Express gratitude during formal opportunities such as annual reviews, holiday gatherings, or routine meetings. During annual reviews, gratitude can be memorialized in writing as a part of the employee's permanent record. This can become evidence that helps support promotion decisions. Expressions of gratitude by providing holiday and other social gatherings serve as an emphatic reminder to team members they are appreciated and valued. The event truly becomes a celebration of joy. Every organization needs at least a minimum number of meetings for members to coordinate their efforts, communicate needs, and plan for the future. These meetings should never be "oral emails." However, they can be effective times to remind team members they are valued and appreciated.

CASE STUDY

Dr. Maria Ortega was selected by the dean of the college to be the new department chair. Her department has not had a department meeting during the tenure of her recently retired predecessor. The senior faculty are not interested in providing leadership to the department since they are in the twilight of their careers. They are no longer focused on promotions and their motivation levels aren't what they used to be. The junior faculty are eager to kick-start their careers, but there is nothing in place to provide them with any mentoring or induction into the department. To make matters worse, the department faculty are housed in three separate locations. Rarely are faculty members who have offices in one location seen in either of the other two locations.

The existing faculty provide a variety of challenges for Dr. Ortega. One faculty member, Dr. John Cook, was recently removed from two different university committees because he was so disruptive to their work. In addition, Dr. Cook refused to cooperate with several recent initiatives the department agreed to undertake. Another faculty member, Dr. Lynn Dorsey, a senior member of the faculty, has told the department chair she "doesn't have time for scholarship, university committees, or department work" this year. Two of the senior faculty members do not like one another and are not hesitant to show it. Still another faculty member won a lawsuit against the university that has created divisions within the department.

In her first meeting with the dean, Dr. Ortega is told that she must lead the department through several initiatives during her first year, including implementing new technology needed for research in her department, preparing a strategic plan for the department that aligns with the university's strategic plan, and developing a strategy for increasing the department's student enrollment by at least 15%. If you were Dr. Ortega, how would you approach your new job?

DISCUSSION QUESTIONS

1. How would you begin the process of developing trust in your department?
2. How would each of the three phases of the *Peopled Leadership* model help you address the challenges you face as the new leader of the department?
3. How would Maslow's hierarchy of needs inform your work? What about Adler's work?
4. Discuss how the research into gratitude could help you move this department from disfunction to transformed.

REFERENCES

Adler, A. (1956). *The individual psychology of Alfred Adler.* Basic Books.

Algoe, S. B. (2012). Find, remind, and bind: The functions of gratitude in everyday relationships. *Social and Personality Psychology Compass, 6*(6), 455–469.

Algoe, S. B., & Haidt, J. (2009). Witnessing excellence in action: The "other-praising" emotions of elevation, gratitude, and admiration. *Journal of Positive Psychology, 4*(2), 105–127.

Algoe, S. B., Haidt, J., & Gable, S. L. (2008). Beyond reciprocity: Gratitude and relationships in everyday life. *Emotion, 8*(3), 425–429.

Bartell, N., & Bartell K. (2016). *Radiant-leadership-model.* Bartell & Bartell. https://bartellbartell.com/home/attachment/radiant-leadership-model/

Bartlett, M. Y., Valdesolo, P., & Arpin, S. N. (2020). The paradox of power: The relationship between self-esteem and gratitude. *Journal of Social Psychology, 160*(1), 27–38.

Cameron, K. S., & Quinn, R. E. (2011). *Diagnosing and changing organizational culture* (3rd ed.). Jossey-Bass.

Covey, S. M. R. (2022). *Trust and inspire: How truly great leaders unleash greatness in others.* Simon & Schuster.

Dewar, K. (2021). *A good little reminder about gratitude.* Counselwise. https://counselwise.ca/good-little-reminder-gratitude/

Emmons, R. A., & Stern, R. (2013). Gratitude as a psychotherapeutic intervention. *Journal of Clinical Psychology, 69*(8), 846–855.

Goldstein, K. (1963a). *Human nature in light of psychopathology.* Schocken.

Goldstein, K. (1963b). *The organism: A holistic approach to biology derived from pathological data on man.* Beacon Press.

Greenleaf, R. K. (1977). *Servant leadership: A journey into the nature of legitimate power and greatness*. Paulist Press.

Gu, Y., Ocampo, J. M., Algoe, S. B., & Oveis, C. (2022). Gratitude expressions improve teammates' cardiovascular stress responses. *Journal of Experimental Psychology, 151*(6), 1–11.

Hersey, P. (1984). *The situational leader.* Center for Leadership Studies.

Jans-Beken, L., & Wong, P. T. (2021). Development and preliminary validation of the existential gratitude scale. *Counseling Psychology Quarterly, 34*(1), 72–86.

Kelley, J. (2018). *The crucible's gift: 5 Lessons from authentic leaders who thrive in adversity.* Executives After Hours.

Koltko-Rivera, M. E. (2006). Rediscovering the late version of Maslow's hierarchy of needs: Self-transcendence and opportunities for theory, research, and unification. *Review of General Psychology, 10*(4), 302–317.

Maslow, A. H. (1943). A theory of human motivation. *Psychological Review, 50*(4), 370–396.

Maslow, A. H. (1969). The farther reaches of human nature. *Journal of Transpersonal Psychology, 1*(1), 1–9.

McGuire, A. P., Szabo, Y. Z., Murphy, K. M., & Erickson, T. M. (2019). Direct and indirect effects of trait and state gratitude on health-related quality of life in a prospective design. *Psychological Reports, 123*(6), 2248–2262.

Wilson, J. T. (2016). Brightening the mind: The impact of practicing gratitude on focus and resilience in learning. *Journal of the Scholarship of Teaching and Learning, 16*(4), 1–13.

Wiseman, L. (2017). *Multipliers: How the best leaders make everyone smarter.* Harper Business.

Zenger, J., & Folkman, J. (2009). *The extraordinary leader: Turning good managers into great leaders.* McGraw-Hill.

Chapter 6

Peopled Leadership and Positive Accountability

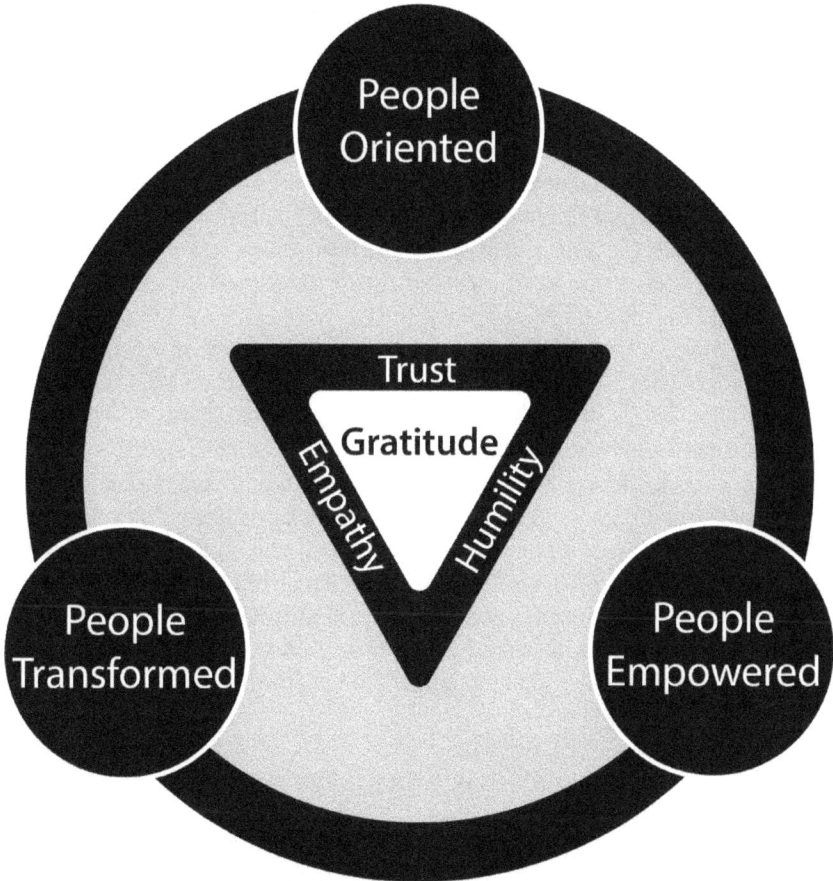

Fig. 6.1. *Peopled Leadership*: Comprehensive Model. *Jack Ousey.*

The 21st century is a challenging time in which to live and work. It is also a challenging time in which to be a leader. Between the lingering effects of a worldwide pandemic, discordant political discourse that doesn't seem to end, and a generally unsettled world, people struggle to find any sense of peace. According to Reinert et al. (2021), nearly one in every five adult Americans is currently experiencing some form of mental illness. That is nearly 50 million Americans. Further, over 11.4 million Americans report experiencing suicidal ideation, an increase of 664,000 from 2021. Over 2.5 million youth experienced a major depressive episode in 2021.

The statistics for American youth are also sobering. Of youth aged 12 to 17, 13.84% reported suffering at least one major depressive episode in the past year. However, this number may be artificially low. Reinert et al. (2021) report that only around half of children afflicted with major depression are diagnosed while still minors. Combined with the more common life occurrences of illness, bereavement, and other challenges, these statistics provide a glimpse of the world in which today's leaders work.

Just recently, the notion of a workplace was turned upside down by a worldwide pandemic. The threat of a particular disease may have subsided to a degree, but the workplace likely remains permanently transformed. Technology, in many occupations, has rendered the concept of commuting to work nearly obsolete. In light of these developments, leadership is a daunting proposition. With the speed at which the 21st-century workplace continues to evolve, how does one lead? *Peopled Leadership* provides a solid answer when we add the element of accountability.

Far too often, accountability is seen as a negative part of the workplace, where leaders are more interested in playing "gotcha" games instead of investing themselves in the growth of those they are entrusted to lead. This chapter discusses the relationship between *Peopled Leadership*, accountability, and successful leadership in the 21st-century workplace. Kenton (2022) defines accountability as "the acceptance of responsibility for one's own actions. It implies a willingness to be transparent, allowing others to observe and evaluate one's performance" (para. 2). In this chapter, the idea of positive accountability is introduced. Positive accountability is a tool through which the leader and organization members work to build trust, practice transparency, and accept constructive feedback on job performance.

ACCOUNTABILITY

Accountability is at the forefront of many organizations: schools, nonprofits, government agencies, and businesses. Accountability, the practice of being held to specified standards, actions, and outcomes, carries with it a great deal of weight. Many people view accountability as suppressive, overburdensome, threatening, and complex. Others view accountability as an avenue for growth, improvement, change, governance, and shared responsibility. Often, the view of accountability, whether it be viewed as positive or negative, is based upon an organization's leadership and commitment to the cause.

Leaders need to acknowledge that members of the organization will approach accountability from different viewpoints, which often stem from a lack of understanding of the accountability model or the consequential nature of accountability. These differing viewpoints are part of a people-centered, open system. Peopled leaders recognize this facet of working with others and approach accountability differently as they seek to create cohesion in support of organizational success and compliance. They also actively seek ways to create a positive accountability culture and message that accountability is good for members of the organization, propels the organization to achieve set goals, and is a way to move the field forward.

Peopled leaders practice positive accountability. Frederick et al. (2016) define accountability as "regular, positive steps to maintain proactive connections with followers" (p. 304). When embedded in a trusting, supporting climate, accountability is transformed from being a negative form of power (e.g., coercive) to a positive form of power (e.g., reward, referent, and expert). Wood and Winston (2005) define accountability as

> the leader's willing acceptance of the responsibilities inherent in the leadership position to serve the well-being of the organization, implicit or explicit expectation that the leader will be publicly linked to his/her actions, words, or reactions; and the expectation that the leader may be called on to explain his or her beliefs, decisions, commitments, or actions to constituents. (pp. 86–87)

Positive accountability must be embedded in a culture of trust, respect, and mutual care to be possible. Positive accountability requires accountability to oneself first and then to others in the organization and the external constituencies of the organization.

The U.S. Office of Personnel Management (n.d.) provides several positive aspects of accountability:

- improved performance,
- more employee participation and involvement,
- increased feelings of competency,
- increased employee commitment to the work,
- more creativity and innovation, and
- higher employee morale and satisfaction with the work. (para. 2)

Finkelstein (n.d.) outlines that benefits of accountability include:

- trustworthiness, collaboration, and cohesiveness;
- the acceptance of more responsibilities;
- stronger teams;
- effective communication;
- increased motivation, productivity, and efficiency;
- improvement in customer satisfaction; and
- increasing returns. (para. 4)

Peopled leaders share these benefits of accountability and find ways to empower organization members to engage in accountability and share how such measures affect their work and the success of the organization. They then find ways to mitigate some of the burdens of accountability while celebrating the need for accountability to help propel the organization and its members to achieve goals and realize the vision and mission.

There are several strategies peopled leaders can use to support a culture of positive accountability. Zwilling (n.d.) provides several key actions for leaders, which include modeling behaviors, communicating expectations, removing the emotion and relying on data or facts, appropriately delegating power and roles, connecting accountability measures and activities with organizational goals, advocating for and celebrating organization members and success, and allowing for safe and open discussions (para. 5–11). Because people-empowered leaders are focused on people and acknowledge that it takes everyone to meet goals, these leaders focus on these exact activities to create and sustain a positive culture of accountability.

PEOPLED LEADERS AND MARGINAL ORGANIZATION MEMBERS

The principles of *Peopled Leadership* are designed to produce organization members who feel valued and respected and who are self-starting and motivated and want to contribute their very best to the organization. This kind of organization member invests efforts in building and maintaining a people-oriented work climate, completes tasks in a timely fashion, and approaches work with an organization-first attitude. Unfortunately, no leadership model is foolproof. Despite the best of efforts of the finest leaders, there are team members whose performance is marginal at best and that require individual change to become productive members. Balancing the critical conversations with the difficulties of navigating an inadequate market for employees is a necessary skill of peopled leaders.

In his book *What Great Principals Do Differently*, Whitaker (2012) suggests that there are two ways to significantly improve a school: get better teachers or improve the teachers you have. This principle is applicable to any organization. This principle is applicable to all organizational settings. Unfortunately, too many leaders prefer to "dance around" marginal team members because confronting them can be difficult. Indeed, McEwan-Adkins (2005, p. 120) indicates that leaders sometimes tolerate ineffective workers because they know that confronting them will be "cognitively demanding, emotionally draining, and physically exhausting."

Bossidy et al. (2002) stated that "nonperforming people are essentially those who aren't meeting their desired goals. They're unable on a regular basis to accomplish what they're responsible for . . . and must be dealt with fairly and quickly" (p. 164). Using the context of schools, Zepeda (2017) explains:

> Dealing with a marginal teacher is one of the most difficult situations a supervisor faces. Confronting marginal teaching will test the mettle of any administrator. Addressing marginal teaching is neither easy nor comfortable for the supervisor or the teacher. (p. 316)

However, these types of conversations are critical for organizational success. Most employees want to know where they stand, and although conversations of this nature are problematic, they do not have to be viewed as an attack on the person. According to DuFour and Eaker (1998, p. 113), "confrontation is not synonymous with personal attack," and leaders are advised to develop a plan of action quickly to ensure that people are held accountable for their actions.

In addition to the dilemma of knowing you need to speak with people about their job performance is the added concern about saying the wrong thing or saying something that is not appropriate, either legally or professionally. Ultimately, the goal of this kind of conference with employees is designed to get them to see the need to improve their output while remaining positive and upbeat about their ability to do so. Clearly defined expectations should be documented and shared so there is no doubt about what is expected. A record of the meeting should also be included in the employees' personnel file for legal documentation that an attempt was made to address concerns that arose during the performance of duties relating to their position (Zepeda, 2017, p. 330).

Since peopled leaders are focused on the emotional and mental needs of their people, they are careful to critique performance and not the person. The peopled leader asks for improvements in performance and necessary changes in behavior but does so without demeaning or undercutting the worth of the organization member. The peopled leader seeks to facilitate necessary changes while simultaneously building up the worth of the individuals with reminders of what they bring to the organization.

Contrary to what many people think about leadership in modern organizations, discussions of this nature have been a part of the evolutionary process related to leadership for a long time. Hoy and Miskel (2013) noted that all bureaucracies are characterized by a career orientation and promotion is dependent on the judgment of superiors. According to Bolman and Deal (2003), interpersonal skills and emotional intelligence are crucial because "personal relationships are a central element of daily life in organizations" (p. 168). In a school setting, Zepeda (2007) states it as a fear of focus:

> If you asked a group of teachers why they hesitate to ask their supervisors to focus on an area of concern, the answer would more than likely be fear—specifically, the belief that their supervisors are out to get them. This fear—now practically a tradition in Pre K-12 schools—grows whenever a supervisor supplants supervision with summative evaluation that serves only to comply with state mandates. (p. 77)

Zepeda (2007) goes on to say that the only way to combat this fear is to build trust between teachers and supervisors. Finding common ground is the best way to engender trust that will allow people to "open up" and be willing to be honest about their ideas regarding job performance and how to improve it. In a school setting, this means quality outcomes that improve the lives of children. These same principles apply in other work settings.

Bregman (2018) offers advice for how to handle the difficult conversations that are necessary if improvement is to be realized. His three-part approach is as follows:

1. Identify the problem.
2. State what needs to happen.
3. Offer to help. (p. 212)

Although these types of conversations can be difficult to mitigate, they are crucially important due to the fact that each element of an organization is needed for quality results. Each part is necessary for optimal success. Peopled leaders who have worked to establish trust and to empower their people are best situated to handle these difficult conversations.

Leaders understand that one person can define an entire culture. This should be the peopled leader. However, if a member of the organization wants to establish a competing culture, the team cannot succeed. Henry David Thoreau once said, "The soul grows by subtraction, not addition." At times, the same holds true about organizations. There can come a time when a leader must make the most difficult decision any leader makes, to remove a team member. This decision should never be approached lightly. It should be made only after reasonable efforts have been made to reach and rehabilitate the team member in question. However, the peopled leader understands that accountability to the team includes removing barriers to success, including a recalcitrant member.

KEEPING YOUR FOCUS AS A PEOPLED LEADER

Bill Cowher, former head coach of the Pittsburgh Steelers, understands the nature of confidence. He describes confidence as

> a very fragile thing and it certainly is something that has to start with your mental approach and your ability to respond and stay focused and not allow negative thoughts to enter into your own mind. When you are successful, it's easier to expect success. All of a sudden, it's not there, it becomes more of a challenge.

It takes great confidence to maintain one's focus, particularly in today's environment of vitriol and discontent. Peopled leaders keep the focus on the people, and that includes the leaders themselves. Meeting the needs of the individual members of the organization pays many dividends.

The organization supports and encourages its members to work hard to be their best, work efficiently and strategically, and consistently meet identified and needed outcomes. However, there are great benefits for the leader as well. Because the peopled leader is a multiplier (Wiseman, 2017), the peopled leader tends to experience reduced levels of stress. There are more people actively engaged in planning, problem solving, and carrying out needed tasks. Peopled leaders also experience organizational and individual productivity at levels never before achieved. Again, this is the multiplier effect. Perhaps the most powerful benefit for leaders is the joy effect. As peopled leaders observe and monitor the daily activities of the organization, they begin to bask in the joy of watching organization members do the problem solving and planning, thus providing solid evidence of the fruits of past labors.

A confident leader tends to instill confidence in others. Team members have the confidence to take calculated risks. They do not shy away from hard work since they are committed to the success of the organization. They believe they can be successful and quite often, they are. Confident organization members help instill confidence in each other. They look for ways to support and help each other, thereby strengthening bonds between members and the organization.

Peopled leaders also admit their mistakes. They are human and fail their organizations from time to time. To continue nurturing a climate of trust, peopled leaders must be up front with their own failings. The ability to admit one's mistakes is a natural result of being a humble leader (see chapter 3).

In the seminal work *Supervisors and Teachers: A Private Cold War*, Blumberg (1980) addresses the difficult nature of working with persons difficult to lead. After providing a list of suggestions to improve the relationship between teachers and supervisors, Blumberg writes:

> It would be foolhardy to suggest that any one of these ideas or any combination of them would guarantee a "New Jerusalem" in supervisor-teacher relationships. They are small steps in need of continual reinforcement. There might, however, be an added bonus: engaging in them might encourage supervisors and teachers to think and talk openly about a couple of subjects that rarely seem to be discussed—themselves and their school as a place to work. (pp. 247–248)

It is this kind of conversation that is the hallmark of peopled leaders.

A CODA FOR PEOPLED LEADERS

Few would argue the challenges of leadership have never been greater than they are in the 21st century. Deepening divisions in society compounded by an ever-increasing load of information (misinformation and disinformation too!) coming from too many directions to count. The need for peopled leaders is critical. However, to be a peopled leader, one must first put into action with oneself those practices discussed throughout this book that are necessary to support the needs of the members of the organization. Peopled leaders remember they, too, are members, and they have the same needs as everyone else. This Coda for Peopled Leaders provides practical guidance for how peopled leaders go about ensuring their own self-care.

Centering Oneself for Leadership

Leadership is hard. The reality of leadership means giving of oneself to organization members, the cause of the organization, and the people and systems the organization impacts, all of which can be daunting. Leaders often find themselves in the midst of their own professional, health, family, spiritual, and personal struggles. Yet for most leaders, the minute they walk in the building they are like a light switch; they must be on for everyone, even if they feel like being in the dark.

Today's leadership roles carry so many challenges. Mental health issues of organization members, inflation and budgetary concerns, exceptions of stakeholders, consequential policies and accountability initiatives, technology and media impacts, and a host of other challenges. So how do leaders do it all? How do they avoid burnout? How do they take care of themselves and model that it is important to find a centered place in the middle of what sometimes can seem to be chaos?

Peopled leaders rely on three behaviors to stay present, centered, and ready for the challenges of leadership. These three behaviors are humility, centering acts, and self-compassion. Peopled leaders are humble enough to recognize they may be struggling and model that it is okay to struggle, ask for help, and lean on fellow organization members. Quest (2011) provides that centered leaders find meaning in work, convert fear and anxiety into opportunities, make and use community and connections, and take necessary risks (para. 1). Such leaders know they are invaluable to the organization and think deeply about how to be more impactful and avoid burnout so that they may continue to serve the organization.

Centering oneself is reliant on emotional intelligence, positive self-talk, prioritizing work, finding peace, practicing life–work balance, actualizing self-forgiveness, being transparent, and looking accurately in the mirror. Neff (2003) provides a definition of self-compassion that is an integral part of centering oneself. Neff argues that self-compassion in not distinguishable from the general definition of compassion and provides:

> Compassion involves being open to and moved by the suffering of others, so that one desires to ease their suffering. It also involves offering others patience, kindness and nonjudgmental understanding, recognizing that all humans are imperfect and make mistakes. Similarly, self-compassion involves being open to and moved by one's own suffering, experiencing feelings of caring and kindness toward oneself, taking an understanding, nonjudgmental attitude toward one's inadequacies and failures, and recognizing that one's own experience is part of the common human experience. (p. 224)

The ability to be humble, keep centered, and be compassionate with oneself is humbling and a central component of peopled leaders.

Self-Care for Peopled Leaders

We take the time here to emphasize the importance of leaders preserving their own physical, mental, emotional, and spiritual well-being. It is impossible to lead an organization of any size to quality results without maintaining a regimen that leads to excellent physical and mental health. What leaders need to realize is that these two concerns are not static; they require daily attention in order to be "at your best." As a result, a careful self-inventory is required that can serve as a "checkup from the neck up" as you consider if specific areas are in need of change.

At the top of this list is sleep. Getting ample sleep every night allows peopled leaders to perform at their best. In *Titan* by Ron Chernow, Rockefeller says that "for years on end I never had a solid night's sleep, worrying about how it was to come out. . . . I tossed about in bed night after night worrying over the outcome." At one point in his life, Rockefeller lost all his hair as well as the hair on both eyebrows due to the enormous stress in his life. Sufficient hours of sleep on a consistent basis is critical for optimal performance.

From time to time, leaders will experience a night when it is difficult to sleep due to the inability to disengage from the work and get their mind off the problems they encounter. This is normal. What is not normal is when leaders are trying to make it on two to four hours of sleep for several nights in a row. Peopled leaders will never be at their best without adequate sleep because this is an important part of the healing process that your body goes through in a daily cycle. Sleep not only helps the body heal; it helps the mind heal as well.

In addition to sleep, diet and exercise are two key components of good health and must be monitored closely. During the aging process, the body changes and physical fitness begins to diminish. Thirty minutes of vigorous exercise at least three days a week is a good start toward getting the exercise you need to be at your best. Finding out which foods to avoid and which foods to get more of and which foods provide for healing, help with rest/sleep, help with digestion, and help with reducing weight if that is a problem helps as leaders get older. The old saying "You are what you eat" is very accurate, and careful consideration of one's diet will help with getting the nutritional requirements for good overall health.

For example, pistachios are a good source of natural melatonin as well as other nutrients. Melatonin is something your body needs to help with sleep. By adding this member of the nut family to the regular diet, leaders may be helping to get the essentials needed for a quality diet and to aid in sleep.

Since the onset of the COVID-19 pandemic, mental health issues have become much more prevalent, causing an increased number of people to struggle with the demands of their jobs. Mental health is an area that must be considered for a leader to be effective. Closely related to the area of mental health is emotional well-being because personal relationships are crucial to feeling loved and cared for. Friendships are forged through adversity, and having someone you can talk to about any concern is necessary for good emotional health.

Lastly, humans are spiritual beings, and as such, we need help being guided along a path that is leading to a good result. The most important area to consider here is scripture. For example, the Holy Bible is filled with encouraging thoughts, stories, and advice about how to handle life's most difficult situations. In Proverbs 3:5–6, God implores us to "Trust in The Lord with all your heart and lean not unto thine own understanding. In all your ways, acknowledge Him and He will direct your path." This is just one of the numerous scriptures that help leaders realize that they are not alone when leading their organizations. Leadership, by the very nature of it, can be lonely and isolating. The view from the top is sometimes disturbing and can lead to self-doubt about whether you have the internal fortitude to meet the demands of the job.

At times like that, it is comforting to know that there are resources available. Prayer and meditation can be essential for all leaders for spiritual centering. These practices can help the peopled leader make needed change, or at the very least, it may change leaders to where they can see where they have made a mistake and go about correcting it. Psalms 34:15 provides wonderful encouragement to pray: "The eyes of The Lord are on the righteous and His ears are open to their cry for help."

Setting Priorities

The demands of leadership are never-ending. In the context of 21st-century challenges, those demands are more daunting. Zepeda et al. (2022) remind us that successful leaders understand that "Support, care, and safety are vital" to any organization and further, that organization members "have a vital need of care and to feel safe both physically and emotionally. A culture of care is created when leaders serve as role models of care, engage in personal and professional conversations, and provide opportunities for others to practice care" (p. 174). Trust, humility, empathy, and gratitude are all key tools for the peopled leader to achieve organizational success in today's atmosphere of uncertainty and contention. People need stability across multiple levels of their lives, and peopled leaders can provide that foundation.

One of the most basic needs of human beings is the need to belong (Maslow, 1943). The *Peopled Leadership* model is designed to ensure this need is met on an ongoing basis. Zepeda et al. (2022) observed, "Everyone wants to feel they belong, that they are valued, and that they are a member of a community. . . . A culture with a strong sense of belonging built through relationships helps . . . bring meaning to [organization members'] work, increases their engagement in the profession, supports professional growth, and increases their sense of efficacy" (p. 174). As discussed previously in this coda, peopled leaders set the stage for this work by centering themselves through carefully designed and faithfully carried out self-care. One last key to that process is the ability to set and maintain priorities.

A common idiom based on military tactics is the age-old question, "Is this a hill you want to die on?" Removing the military connotation, this is really a question of priorities. Peopled leaders keep their eyes on the priorities of the organization and its members. Buried within this adage, are various questions about each situation, such as "What are the chances of success?" "Will this initiative get us closer to our desired outcomes?" and "Is pursuing this avenue cost- effective?" In addition to these questions, peopled leaders understand that the ultimate question is, "Is this initiative expending organizational resources in a way that will advance the physical, social, mental, emotional, and spiritual health of the organization and its members?"

Chances of Success

In today's world, resources are scarce and therefore, precious commodities. Organization members depend on leaders to provide direction that will provide them individually and the organization as a collective the greatest chance of success. Peopled leaders also view success in terms of individual and organizational growth in addition to goal attainment.

Another meaning of the "hill" metaphor requires leaders to decide if they wish to insist on their own point of view in a particular situation. Peopled leaders have the skill to provide members of the organization opportunities to offer their points of view but also to know when the leader's point of view must predominate. One hallmark of strong leaders is the ability to make decisions they must and when possible and appropriate, to delegate other decisions. Regardless, a true peopled leader stands by the decisions made.

Getting Closer to Desired Outcomes and Cost- Effectiveness

Every decision leaders make needs to be calculated to move the organization closer to achieving its desired outcomes. Are resources being used properly, including human resources? Is there a more efficient means to achieve the outcome. In addition to these questions, the peopled leader also examines any potential risks. Empowered and transformed organizations are composed of members who think "out of the box" to find solutions to ever-evolving challenges. They are not averse to taking calculated risks that could bring success, both personally and to the organization. However, those risks must be carefully weighed to ensure the highest probability of success and the potential for negative results is minimized. Leaders skilled at making these kinds of decisions are peopled leaders who are always monitoring the well-being of their team members.

ADDRESSING THE ULTIMATE QUESTION

The peopled leader knows that achieving outcomes in ways detrimental to the well-being of team members is also detrimental to the well-being of the organization. In every decision, the true bottom line for peopled leaders is whether or not their leadership is resulting in providing a workplace climate that supports and nurtures the physical, social, mental, emotional, and spiritual well-being of the people. Peopled leadership values and respects people, provides a harbor of support amid the challenges of life, and creates an efficient organization that is made up of members that *want* to achieve and will go above and beyond to do so. Leadership that remains focused on the people creates an organization that solves problems, manages change, and achieves required outcomes.

REFERENCES

Blumberg, A. (1980). *Supervisors and teachers: A private cold war* (2nd ed.). McCutchan.

Bolman, L. G., & Deal, T. E. (2003). *Reframing organizations: Artistry, choice, and leadership* (3rd ed.). Jossey-Bass.

Bossidy, L., Charan, R., & Burck, C. (2002). *Execution: The discipline of getting things done.* Crown Business.

Bregman, P. (2018). Leading with emotional courage: *How to have hard conversations, create accountability, and inspire action on your most important work.* Wiley & Sons.

DuFour, R., & Eaker, R. (1998). *Professional learning communities at work: Best practices for enhancing student achievement.* Solution Tree Press.

Finkelstein, D. (n.d.). *What is positive accountability?* TickThoseBoxes.com. Retrieved August 30, 2022, from https://tickthoseboxes.com.au/what-is-positive-accountability/

Frederick, H. R., Wood, J. A., West, G. R., & Winston, B. E. (2016). The effect of the accountability variables of responsibility, openness, and answerability on authentic leadership. *Journal of Research on Christian Education, 25*(3), 302–316.

Hoy, W. K., & Miskel, C. G. (2013). Educational administration: Theory, research, and practice (9th ed.). McGraw-Hill.

Kenton, W. (2022, July 25). *Accountability: Definition, types, benefits, and example.* Investopedia. https://www.investopedia.com/terms/a/accountability.asp

Maslow, A. H. (1943). A theory of human motivation. *Psychological Review, 50*(4), 370–396.

McEwan-Adkins, E. K. (2005). *How to deal with teachers who are angry, troubled, exhausted, or just plain confused.* Corwin Press.

Neff, K. (2003). The development and validation of a scale to measure self-compassion. *Self and Identity, 2*(3), 223–250.

Quest, L. (2011, August 22). How to be a "centered" leader. *Forbes.* https://www.forbes
.com/sites/lisaquast/2011/08/22/are-you-a-centered-leader/?sh=1309b1ff3c22

Reinert, M., Fritze, D., & Nguyen, T. (2021, October 1). *The state of mental health in
America 2022.* Mental Health America.

U.S. Office of Personnel Management. (n.d.). *Policy, data, oversite performance
management: Accountability can have positive results.* Retrieved August 30,
2022, from https://www.opm.gov/policy-data-oversight/performance-management
/reference-materials/more-topics/accountability-can-have-positive-results

Whitaker, T. (2012). *What great principals do differently: 18 Things that matter most.*
Routledge.

Wiseman, L. (2017). *Multipliers: How the very best leaders make everyone smarter.*
HarperCollins.

Wood, J. A., & Winston, B. E. (2005). Toward a new understanding of leader accountability: Defining a critical construct. *Journal of Leadership & Organizational
Studies, 11*(3), 84–94.

Zepeda, S. J. (2007). *Instructional supervision: Applying tools and concepts* (2nd
ed.). Eye on Education.

Zepeda, S. J. (2017). *Instructional supervision: Applying tools and concepts* (4th ed.).
Routledge.

Zepeda, S. J., Lanoue, P. D., Rivera, G. M., & Shafer, D. R. (2022). *Leading school
culture through teacher voice and agency.* Routledge.

Zwilling, M. (n.d.). 7 Keys to developing a positive accountability culture in your
organization: Responsibilities and accountability are required for leadership success in any business. *Inc.* Retrieved August 28, 2022, from https://www.inc.com
/martin-zwilling/7-keys-to-developing-a-positive-accountability-culture-in-your
-organization.html

Index

accountability, 4; autonomy and, 36; benefits of, 88; in COVID-19 pandemic, 86; defined, 86–87; of marginal organization members, 88–91; in *Peopled Leadership*, 85–97; in People Empowered phase, 40; positive aspects of, 87; in trust, 22; trust and, 87

achievement gap, 4

Adler, A., 70–71

admiration, 77

Algoe, S. B., 76, 77–78, 80

analysis, in problem-solving, 62

Auster, E. R., 19

authenticity: humility and, 35; in People Empowered phase, 32; in People Oriented phase, 19

authority: defined, 41; in People Empowered phase, 40–44, *41*

autonomy: defined, 36; gratitude and, 80; listening and, 59; in People Empowered phase, 35–37, 80

Baird, J., 62

Bartlett, M. Y., 76

belonging: in community, 70–71; in organizational culture, 95

Bencsik, A., 6

Bier, M., 40

Blanchard, K., 17, 18, 62

Bloom, B., 61, 62

Blumberg, A., 92

Bolman, L. G., 90

Bossidy, L., 89

Bramlett, C. H., 56

Brandeis, Louis, 22

Brandt, D., 56

Bregman, P., 90

Buckingham, M., 61

burnout, 52

Caredda, S., xi

Chambers, R., 20

change management, 56–58

Chaudhary, P., 54–55

Chernow, Ron, 94

Chiu, T., 34–35

coercive power, 42

Coffman, C., 61

collaboration, 5; accountability and, 88; in community, 71; gratitude and, 81; in leadership, 35–36; in People Empowered phase, 32; in People Oriented phase, 17; in trust, 8; trust and, 25

Collins, J. C., 63

commitment: accountability and, 87; to empowerment, 36; in

www.ingramcontent.com/pod-product-compliance
Lightning Source LLC
Chambersburg PA
CBHW021603210326
41599CB00010B/581